'TILL HE COMES

By Ted Merritt

Contents

Acknowledgements..7

Preface..8

Introduction..10

Part I: How We Can Know We Are in the End Times..................14

1: Why Study Bible Prophecy?...15

2: How Do We Know We're in the Last Days?..........................19

3: Israel is the Key...27

4: Two More Signs...36

Part II: The Rapture of the Church..42

5: Introduction to the "Catching Away"..................................43

6: Pretribulationism..46

7: Posttribulationism..53

8: Midtribulationism...55

9: Partial Rapture...57

10: Pre-Wrath..60

Part III: The Tribulation..65

11: Why Will There Be a Tribulation?....................................66

12: A Time of Transition..70

13: When the Church Goes to Heaven....................................75

14: Worship Before the Throne..82

15: The First Seal, the Man of Sin..91

16: Ten Kingdoms and Two Witnesses..95

17: Hell Pays a Visit..99

18: The 144,000..105

19: The Trumpet Judgments...108

20: The Halfway Point..116

21: The Seven Bowls..124

Part IV: The Second Coming and the Millennium.........................132

22: Armageddon...133

23: The Case for a Future Millennium..139

24: Internal Clocks...146

25: We Shall (not) All be Changed..152

26: The Millennium as Seen Through the Eyes of Isaiah..............156

27: The Devil's Swan Song..162

28: The Fate of the Devil and His Minions......................................167

29: The Second Death...172

30: Global Warming...176

31: We Shall Overcome...182

32: The New Jerusalem...188

33: His Reward is with Him..195

Part V: The Seventieth Week of Daniel..202

34: Introduction to Daniel's Eschatology..203

35: The Prayer that Brings the Prophecy..205

36: An Overview of the Seventy Weeks...208

37: On Earth as it is in Heaven	216
38: The Sealing of Prophecy	221
39: The First Sixty-Nine Weeks	223
40: Messiah is Cut Off	226
41: The Coming Flood	230
42: The Abomination of Desolation	236
43: Time, Times, and Half a Time	242
44: The Two Witnesses	247
45: The Tribulation Temple	253
46: Christ's Victory and Antichrist's Doom	258
Epilogue	266
Appendix A	269
Appendix B	270
Bibliography	271

Ted Merritt

Mark 13:24-26

'TILL HE COMES

A Look at the Return of Jesus and the End of the

World

"And let us consider one another in order to stir up love and good works, not forsaking the assembling of ourselves together, as is the manner of some, but exhorting one another, and so much the more as you see the Day approaching" – Heb. 10:24-25

Acknowledgments

To my magnificent and beautiful wife, Debbie, I offer my deepest gratitude. Were it not for her, this project never would have gotten off the ground. God used this precious woman to constantly encourage me and to do all the thankless "grunt work" that goes into an undertaking of this magnitude. She was my editor and proofreader, but more than that she served me by doing what she does best: she was my best friend, cheerleader, and confidant. Thanks, honey, for everything!

Thanks go out also to those who planted the seed in my head to try something I never thought I'd succeed in doing. The idea for me to write and publish a book most assuredly did not originate with me! To Chris Cain, Nick and LeAndre Davis, Tenna Garrett, Sharon Gricol, Chuck Korte, Jaimie Krycho, Richard Manning, Patrick Mooney, Al and Wendy Silberstein, David Turner, and Terry and Tandy Warren, I am indebted to you for having seen an opportunity for God to use me in this way.

Finally, and most important, I give all thanks and praise to my Savior and Lord, Jesus Christ. To Him be all honor and glory and praise, for without Him I would still be dead in my trespasses and sins. He is the coming King of kings and Lord of lords, and may His name be magnified by this work.

Soli deo gloria!

Preface

Welcome to the End Times! Not a pleasant thought, I know, considering the fact that just about the only thing that most Christians can agree on when it comes to the so-called "Last Days" is that the ride from here to the end will be a rough one. As a Christian and student of Bible prophecy, I have to tell you that I believe we are indeed approaching the very last hours of history, and that things will only get worse from here on out until, well, UNTIL HE COMES.

I've opened quite a can of worms here, haven't I? I'm sure that these bold remarks will bring a flood of questions. Just who is "He," the One of whom I'm speaking that is coming one day? That would be none other than the Lamb of God, the Lord of Glory, Jesus Christ. Next question: How do I know that He's actually coming back? Another question: How do I know we're living in the last days? And another: How do I know that the world is going to keep on getting worse until "He" comes? Well, in the pages that follow, I hope to answer these questions as satisfactorily as space will allow. So, if you dare, come take a trip with me into the future, and let's find out how much we can know and understand about the days to come.

There are a couple of things I need to tell you before we begin. First, I will be using one primary source for everything in this work, and (naturally!) is the Bible. The next thing you need to know is that I've divided this book into five parts. We'll start by taking a look at the world around us and comparing some of the biggest events of recent history with what the Bible has to say about them in relation to God's timeline for the future. The second portion will deal with a singular event, the Rapture of the Church. There are several views among dispensational Christians regarding the timing of the Rapture. Some say it will occur before the Tribulation begins, while others argue that the Rapture will take place during the Tribulation or even at the end of it. (The Tribulation is a period of seven years that will be marked by the most severe judgments God has ever poured out upon the earth.)

Third, we'll discuss the Tribulation itself. In this section, we'll discuss personages with titles like "Antichrist," "False Prophet," and "witnesses." We will also be examining the aforementioned judgments that are described in the book of Revelation. In the fourth part, we'll take a look at the Second Coming of the Lord Jesus as well as the events that follow. His return will usher in a 1,000-year period of global peace and prosperity known as the "Millennial Kingdom," which will ultimately give way to the eternal future in a New Heaven and a New Earth for all of the redeemed of God, and an eternity of suffering in the lake of fire for those who rejected Christ as their Savior and Lord. The fifth and final portion of the book is dedicated to what's often called the "Seventieth Week of Daniel," which is found in Dan. 9:24-27. These four verses are the lynchpin of end-time prophecy. To have an understanding of this passage is to have a great start on grasping the whole of biblical eschatology.

If you're ready, turn the page and let's take this journey together into the future, a future that starts here and will carry us to the day He comes!

Introduction

Have you ever heard of "moksha"? How about "nirvana"? You've probably heard of the latter, which is to the Buddhist what heaven is to the Christian. Moksha is essentially the Hindu version of Nirvana. In these two religions (Buddhism and Hinduism), which are the most widely practiced of all the Eastern belief systems, it is the goal of the practitioner to reach the point where they are no longer subject to the cycle of birth, death, and rebirth. You see, these Oriental philosophies teach that life is circular, or cyclical. People are born, they live, they die, and then they return as someone (or something) else, dependent on how good or bad they were in the previous life. This is a doctrine known as transmigration. Their ultimate goal is to finally be "good enough" to break that cycle and enter into a state of a sort of blissful nothingness, which is often compared to the blowing out of a candle.

Buddhists and Hindus both embrace an eschatology (a study or system of beliefs related to the End Times) that will include moral decay, but even the eons of time will recycle and begin again for billions of years into the future. They have no concrete belief in an end to the universe. For them, time is such that history is forever and eternally repeating itself.

Some Christians see time in this way, too. They're called "preterists." Those who hold to this doctrine believe that all Bible prophecy, including all end-time prophecies (e.g. the resurrection of the dead, the Second Coming of Jesus, and the Judgments), are either to be taken metaphorically or they took place in A.D. 70 with the destruction of Jerusalem. A much larger group of people, known as "partial preterists," believe that the world-ending events will occur at some unknown time in the future, but all other prophetic events have been fulfilled.

The remainder of Christianity is divided into three predominant groups. One group, known as "amillennialists," interprets the thousand-year period described in Rev. 20:1-6 as being allegorical. They teach that Jesus is presently reigning on the earth through His church, and He will come at the end of this period to usher in the final age, eternity itself.

A second category of Christians is made up of people who call themselves "postmillennialists." They believe that the church will be responsible for bringing in a worldwide Golden Age, at the end of which will be the Second Coming (which some theologians call the "Parousia," or "appearing"). Their belief system is built around the idea that the church has been given the divine assignment of making the world a good enough place for the Lord to come and rule. However, the world has hardly been improving, so this view has fallen into disfavor in recent decades.

The third and final eschatological view is called "premillennialism." This is where I pitch my tent. Premillennialists believe that Jesus will return prior to the 1,000-year age to come (what is known as the "Millennium"), set up His kingdom, and all believers of all the ages will rule the world with Him. It's a fair question to ask: Where does this belief system originate? It comes from the passage I just mentioned, Rev. 20:1-6. I am a premillennialist because I believe that this view is precisely what the Bible teaches. Unlike the Buddhist and the Hindu, I believe that time is not cyclical. It is linear, headed toward a definite end.

The other Christian viewpoints that I just mentioned, particularly the preterist view, are creating what I like to call "prophetic agnostics." I call them that because of their insistence that we don't have enough information in the Bible to know when the end will come. The result of this is that Satan can use such notions to steal the joy of the believer. If we can't have any idea whatsoever of when our Lord will come or, worse, we believe He will never physically return, that takes away the very blessed hope that God has expressly told us we're to be looking for (Tit. 2:11-13). By the way, I inserted a chart at the end of this book. Drawn by my wife, this diagram provides a succinct illustration of what each of the aforementioned views looks like. It can be found in Appendix A on page 269.

As I noted in the preface, we will look at the subject of this coming End of Days by going through the following topics: (1) Current events and what the Bible says about them in relation to the time of the end; (2) The Rapture and whether it will take place before, during, or after the Tribulation; (3) The seven-year Tribulation itself; (4) The Second Coming, the Millennium, and the Eternal State; and (5) The "Seventieth Week" of Daniel, which is found in Dan. 9:24-27.

I believe it's important for us to know and understand the signs of our times, because that makes us better equipped to minister to others. There is little doubt that we are in the closing hours of history. One reason I know that is because of what we read in II Pet. 3:3-4: "...Scoffers will come in the last days, walking according to their own lusts, and saying, 'Where is the promise of His coming? For since the fathers fell asleep, all things continue as they were from the beginning of creation.'" The lost world doesn't believe in the Parousia. For many people, time is cyclical, and they are unable to accurately interpret the signs that we can point to in order for us to draw a different conclusion.

But every time you partake of the Lord's Supper, you are saying that you reject that idea. You're embracing a literal end to the world as we now know it. Don't believe me? Let me prove it to you with the Scripture: "For I received from the Lord that which I also delivered to you: that the Lord Jesus on the same night in which He was betrayed took bread; and when He had given thanks, He broke it and said, 'Take, eat; this is My body which is broken for you; do this in remembrance of Me.' In the same manner He also took the cup after supper, saying, 'This cup is the new covenant in My blood. This do, as often as you drink it, in remembrance of Me.' For as often as you eat this bread and drink this cup, you proclaim the Lord's death <u>'till He comes</u>" (I Cor. 11:23-26, emphasis mine). That, dear friend, is a literal statement, and you can take it to the bank!

Part One

How We Can Know We Are in the End Times

Chapter 1

Why Study Bible Prophecy?

Before we go any further, I think we ought to ask why we should even concern ourselves with studying Bible prophecy. After all, if I'm right, we won't even be on this earth when the Tribulation begins. If that's true, then what difference does it make? Why should we care about things that won't directly affect us? These are valid questions, and they deserve answers. I want to make a case for studying Bible prophecy right now, so we can examine these things together without fear of getting halfway through and then letting doubt creep into our minds as to why we're even bothering to learn this stuff. I would like to give you a list of some of the most important reasons for learning about eschatology and put it to rest before we begin this daunting task. We've asked a loaded question, but it's a very simple one: Why study End Times Bible prophecy? Below are some of my top reasons:

1. <u>It's in the Bible.</u> Roughly 28% of the Bible was prophetic at the time it was written. Many scholars have estimated that there are over 1,000 prophecies in all of Scripture, and some 500 of them have yet to be fulfilled. Since all of the fulfilled prophecies have been fulfilled literally, we can expect that all of the remaining prophecies will likewise be fulfilled literally. Approximately one of every twenty-five verses in the New Testament is in

relation to the Second Coming, and all but four New Testament books mention the return of Jesus.

2. <u>It confirms the legitimacy of the Bible.</u> No other book in all of history has made predictions that came true like the Bible has. No other book boldly foretells the future like the Bible does, and this gives us complete confidence in God's Word.

3. <u>It lets us know we're properly interpreting Scripture.</u> When we're able to see world events in light of Scripture and predict accurately how those events will turn out, we can know we're on the right track. We're not perfect, but God's Word is!

4. <u>It's an encouragement for us to know the future.</u> Unsaved people have no understanding of what's coming, but we can and should know the signs of our times. This keeps us grounded in the fact that as bad as things are, there's a day coming when all will be made right.

5. <u>When we have an idea about things to come, we can order our lives accordingly.</u> When we are armed with knowledge about the future, we're able to make better decisions about how to invest our time and resources.

6. <u>It aids in evangelizing the lost.</u> When we have answers that help make sense of this world gone mad, lost people are able to see the veracity of the Bible for themselves. This also gives us standing and credibility with our friends who don't know the Lord.

7. <u>It gives us a sense of urgency.</u> Knowing that the time could be short should propel us to plead with our unsaved loved ones with more zeal.

8. <u>Since all fulfilled prophecies were literally fulfilled, we know that all future prophecies will likewise be fulfilled literally.</u> (This observation was made as part of my first point above.) This, in turn, helps us guard against misinterpreting Scripture.

9. <u>Understanding the future helps us better understand the present.</u> While much of the world is panicking over calamities and seemingly unexplainable events, we are able to rest in the fact that God has a purpose in all things (and we can often see where He's headed when we analyze these situations).

10. <u>It causes us to put our faith in God rather than men.</u> No institution, no government, no human being is able to fix the mess we're in. But we know and love the Creator of all things, and we know that He works all things together for good to those who love Him.

11. <u>It helps us understand other parts of Scripture better.</u> This is one of those "hip bone's connected to the leg bone" principles. When people understand prophecies that are yet to be fulfilled, they will inherently gain a clearer understanding of the rest of the Bible, even those portions that aren't necessarily prophetic (cf. Acts 20:27).

I want to insert a very important point here. To put it in the form of another question, what is the most important subject surrounding the Bible's unfulfilled prophecies? I would argue that the answer is, beyond all doubt, the Second Coming. If Jesus doesn't return, He lied, because He promised us that He would. His return is our "blessed hope" (Tit. 2:13)! Read Luke 4:16-21; Isa. 61:1-2a. Jesus said in Luke that He was fulfilling the prophecy of Isaiah right then. Now read Isa. 61:2b-4. It's obvious that Jesus hasn't completely carried out His entire assignment. But there is coming a day when He will! We are to take comfort in this truth; in fact, we should meditate day and night on the coming of our Lord. Knowing this one thing will help us keep our sanity more than any other single thought we can have.

Chapter 2

How Do We Know We're in the Last Days?

The Bible has much to say about what the last days will be like, so let's take a look at several of them. First, consider the words of the angel to Daniel. In Daniel 12, the prophet is receiving a prophecy of the end time, and in v. 4, he is given these special instructions: "But you, Daniel, shut up the words, and seal the book until the time of the end; many shall run to and fro, and knowledge shall increase". The whole world is running back and forth at a frenetic pace, and the amount of information we receive is out of control. You probably know people who are virtually hooked on the news (which, let's face it, is not really news anymore). If we were to take the news off the air, there would be "news junkies" everywhere suffering major withdrawals!

Notice also that the words of Daniel's prophecy were to be "sealed up" (i.e. their meaning was to be kept a secret) until the time of the end. This is a recurring theme for the book of Daniel, as 8:26 and 9:24 both speak of "sealing up" visions and prophecies. Daniel was told several times that he wouldn't understand these prophetic visions the angel had imparted to him, but it was a different story for John. In Rev. 22:10, an angel tells John: "Do not seal the words of the prophecy of this book, for the time is at hand." One way we can know that we're in the end times is that these prophetic books are starting to make sense in ways they never have before.

To further illustrate this, let me give you an example of just how much our knowledge is "increasing." It's been estimated that in Jesus' day, the total amount of information to which the average person would be exposed over the course of his entire life is about the same amount of information that you and I typically receive in one daily newspaper! I recently read about an experiment that was conducted by researchers at the University of California-Berkeley back at the turn of the new century. The people conducting the experiment recorded all the information that was spat out by the world's news media over the course of the calendar year 2000. They determined that the total production of news disseminated in that year amounted to 37,000 times more information than was contained in the entire Library of Congress! They repeated the study in 2003, and they calculated that the quantity of information being released was growing by 66% every single year! [1]

So the speed at which we're exposed to information is certainly a sign that the book of Daniel says to look for as an end-time event. Second, the Bible predicts that the nation of Israel will be gathered back into her land near the time we can expect our Lord to return to earth. Read Ezek. 36:24-36, which is a prophecy that was written around 550 B.C. Notice that only one part of this prophecy has been fulfilled; the Jews have been returning to their land at a steady pace for quite some time (v. 25), but their Messiah has yet to come and rule over them (v. 24).

A more detailed account of this prophecy is found in the next chapter of Ezekiel, and I want to look at it. Turn to Chapter 37, and read vs. 1-14. This is a two-part prophecy. First, it's the nation being "reborn." Second, it's the nation standing as a single mighty army under God's leadership. The first part is all that's been fulfilled up to now, as Israel exists now as a very secular country.

But please keep reading, to see what is coming in the future. Read vs. 15-28, paying special attention to vs. 21-25. Israel is going to be inhabited by Jews from every tribe, from both the northern and southern kingdoms, and they will again be a united nation. This has never happened since the nation split in ca. 960 B.C., shortly after Solomon died. This prophecy is not completely fulfilled, but with the children of Israel pouring back into their land, we can see this miracle unfolding before our eyes! (As I write this, there are now more Jews in Israel than in any other single country in the world. That's the first time this has happened since their dispersion nearly two thousand years ago.)

By the way, we can also know that this is most assuredly an event that signals the end is upon us. Verse 21 says they'll be gathered back in their land. Verse 22 states that they will be *one nation* and that they'll have a single king. Verse 23 says that God will miraculously clean up the people's act. Verse 24 speaks of David being their king, but is it really David?

If you read Isa. 9:6-7; Jer. 23:5-6, you'll see that the Jews understood that there was a promise that God made to them, that a *descendant* of David would come one day and rule them in peace and righteousness. This promise transfers to the New Testament, where Jesus' line back to David gave Him the pedigree necessary to claim the throne (cf. Matt. 1:1; Luke 1:32; John 7:42; Acts 13:22-23; II Tim. 2:8).

The promise here is that Israel will be back, they'll literally be one nation under God (indivisible!), they'll have a righteous and perfect King, and now (Ezek. 37:25; cf. Isa. 11:11-13) they'll never be forced out of their land again! These events started on May 14, 1948, when Israel regained her statehood, and they will flow into what we call the Millennium. There's no doubt that Israel being back in her own land is an end-time event!

Okay, let's look at a third biblical prophecy. Turn to Daniel 2. Daniel was exiled to Babylon very early in his life, and he answered to King Nebuchadnezzar. In this second chapter, the king had a troubling dream. He demanded of his advisers that they tell him what his dream was and what it meant. They could do neither, so enter Daniel. He told the king both the dream and its interpretation; it was all about a statue. Read Dan. 2:31-44. From head to foot, the empires represented are Babylon (head), Medo-Persia (chest/arms), Greece (belly/thighs), Rome (legs), and revived Rome (feet and toes).

The Roman Empire, over time, fell apart. The western half evaporated in A.D. 476, and the eastern half (the Byzantine Empire) fell in A.D. 1453. According to what we just read in vs. 34-35, these world empires (starting at the feet with the revived Roman Empire) would meet a sudden and final defeat. That has not happened yet. According to vs. 40-43, this revived fourth kingdom is not as unified and therefore not as strong as it was before. This time, it will be strong like iron but also (paradoxically) as fragile as clay.

Now jump ahead a little bit to Daniel 7, where there's another 4-kingdom dream, only this time it is Daniel's vision. Read Dan. 7:7-8, 23-25. These verses are speaking of a single person, the coming Antichrist, who we'll talk about extensively later on. What I want you to see here is that this revived Roman Empire will be divided into ten kingdoms. We know that this must be an end-time prophecy for at least two reasons:

(1) The Roman Empire has never been divided into ten parts; and (2) It has never suffered sudden destruction, but someday it will (Dan. 2:34-35).

But how do we know that's what's happening? Remember, it's important to understand that prophetic events always cast a shadow before they occur. Rome is certainly casting a shadow right now! The European Union can trace its origins back to the 1950s, but it was officially established by the Maastricht Treaty in 1992. It presently represents 28 European nations. Wikipedia says this about the European Union: "The EU has developed a single market through a standardized system of laws that apply in all member states. Within the 'Schengen Area' (which includes 22 EU and 4 non-EU states) passport controls have been abolished. EU policies aim to ensure the free movement of people, goods, services, and capital, enact legislation in justice and home affairs, and maintain common policies on trade, agriculture, fisheries, and regional development.

"The Eurozone, a monetary union, was established in 1999 and came into full force in 2002. It is currently composed of 17 member states. Through the Common Foreign and Security Policy, the EU has developed a role in external relations and defense. Permanent diplomatic missions have been established around the world. The EU is represented at the UN, the WTO (World Trade Organization), the G8, and the G20." [2] So the EU holds in common many "national" characteristics, such as laws, courts, elections, representatives, agriculture, commerce, bureaucracies, and defense. Then there's the Eurodollar, which is the currency of the EU. We can say with confidence that the Roman Empire is making a comeback!

That makes three end-time prophecies having come into sharper focus. Here's a fourth one; go back to Ezekiel. We're going to look at a coalition of forces that will align themselves against Israel. Israel is a democratic republic that is completely surrounded by 22 hostile Arab/Islamic dictatorships that are 640 times her size and 60 times her population. As a little aside, some people say that the Israel of today isn't the "real" Israel. They argue that the occupants of the land aren't really "Jews" because they have no traceable tribal lineage and they are not worshiping in Old Testament fashion. What these folks are apparently failing to recognize is that these Jewish people will soon be worshiping and sacrificing in their very own temple. And as far as it goes with their Jewish pedigrees, somebody needs to tell these Israelis that they're not really Jews, because *they* think they're Jews, and all those angry, jealous Muslims surrounding them and outnumbering them 60-to-1 need to know that those Jews aren't really Jews, because *they* think they're Jews!

Anyway, back to this business of the fourth prophecy that tells us we're in the end times. Read Ezek. 38:1-7. This is a forecast that there will be a coalition of nations or people groups who will come against Israel. We'll get to the part about Israel in a minute, but let's start with the list of nations that will come up against her. In v. 2, we have a prince whose name is "Gog." In this verse, along with 39:1, Gog is explicitly called the prince of Magog, Rosh, Meshech, and Tubal. According to many students of Bible prophecy, Magog and Rosh are areas that are now found in Russia. Meshech, Tubal, Gomer, and Togarmah are all regions found in present-day Turkey. The countries listed in Ezek. 38:5 are Persia, Ethiopia, and Libya. Persia, by the way, is nothing other than modern-day Iran, a name it has held only since 1935.

But the real bully in this situation, the ringleader over all these other countries, has to be Russia. Read Ezek. 38:14-16. Gog is the head honcho, and Magog is the main nation of people that's going to orchestrate this military campaign against Israel.

Let me pause here and say that we know that this is another end-time prophecy. How do we know that? Because that's what the Bible says! "After many days you will be visited. In the *latter years* you will come into the land of those brought back from the sword and gathered from many people on the mountains of

Israel, which had long been desolate; they were brought out of the nations, and now all of them *dwell safely*" (Ezek. 38:8, emphasis mine). This is a companion verse to what we saw a moment ago in vs. 14-16. These people will come up against Israel "in the latter years." The fact that it will be in the end time is obvious, since the Bible explicitly says so. In addition, we know that it will be in the last days because the children of Israel will be back in their land and "dwelling safely." Israel is hardly a safe place right now. Indeed, it hasn't been safe there since the days of Solomon, some 3,000 years ago. But there's coming a day when Israel will be safe, which we shall discuss momentarily.

Before we do that, though, let's finish the thought on this unlikely collection of nations. All we have to do is turn on the news almost any hour of the day, and we'll see something about Russia and Iran cavorting together. The other major player in this appears to be Turkey, although they haven't made a whole lot of noise (yet). But Russia and Iran are most assuredly cozying up to one another, and these other satellite groups appear to be joining in as well.

Now we have four things that tell us we're getting really close to the end: we're running to and fro and increasing in knowledge; Israel is back on the map (against all odds); the Roman Empire is making a comeback; and Middle Eastern nations are aligning with Russia in preparation for an attack against Israel. This fourth observation dovetails into the fifth, the prediction that Israel will be "safe" in her land. In this next chapter, we will zero in on that tiny nation that God loves and the world hates.

Chapter 3

Israel is the Key

There's coming a day prior to the Lord's return when Israel will be rid of its violence, and they will be at peace. Let's look at this end-time clue by revisiting a few verses we read in Chapter Two. Remember, Ezekiel 38 starts out with God stirring Israel's enemies to line up against her; vs. 1-7 gives the list of those enemies. Now read vs. 8-15. Three times in that passage – vs. 8, 11, and 14 – the Bible says that Israel will "dwell safely." One might ask, "How can this be?" Israel is not safe right now. Well, we're going to take a peek into the future for a minute. In order to do that, we're going to also glance at a couple of passages where we're going to spend more time a little later in our study.

We'll look first at the "Seventieth Week" prophecy, found in the last few verses of Daniel 9. Verse 24 is a summary statement of the prophecy, which covers a stretch of 490 years. The first 483 of those years have taken place, but there's one seven-year period that hasn't occurred yet. Verses 25-26 discuss the 483 years that spanned the period from shortly after the prophet wrote this book until the first coming of Messiah. The prophetic message, which climaxes in that final seven years yet future, is the focus of v. 27. Let's read it: "Then he shall confirm a covenant with many for one week; But in the middle of the week he shall bring an end to sacrifice and offering. And on the wing of abominations shall be one who makes desolate, even until the consummation, which is determined, is poured out on the desolate."

I really want to concentrate on that first half of the verse. We're going to spend a good deal more time studying this section of Scripture on down the line, but I want to stop here long enough for us to be made aware that there is a time of peace coming to Israel *before* Jesus returns. This verse starts out by saying that "he" (referring to Antichrist) is going to sign a treaty that's supposed to last "one week." When we take a deeper look at this later, we'll see how we know that "he" is Antichrist.

For now, though, I want to draw your attention to the fact that this treaty is for a "week." That seems like an awfully short period for a treaty, doesn't it? Well, I'm here to tell you that the treaty of which this verse speaks is not going to be for a measly seven days. Some Bible translations render the word "week" as "seven," which is actually a more accurate interpretation of the word. But let's unravel the mystery of this treaty by using the word "week." Go back to Genesis for a minute. Chapter 29 is the story of Jacob, Rachel, Leah, and Laban. Jacob is traveling in search of Laban, who is his uncle. As he draws near to Laban's home, he meets Laban's daughter Rachel and falls in love with her. After talking with Rachel, Jacob is invited to come and stay with Laban. Pick up the action from there, and read Gen. 29:15-28. All right, Jacob works for his Uncle Laban for seven years to earn the right to marry Rachel. But Laban pulls out his own version of "bait and switch," and Jacob ends up getting stuck with Leah.

It's clear that Laban did that to finagle seven more years of cheap labor out of his nephew. We see this in vs. 26-28 (emphasis mine): "And Laban said, 'It must not be done so in our country, to give the younger before the firstborn. Fulfill her *week,* and we will give you this one also for the service which you will serve with me still another *seven years.*' Then Jacob did so and fulfilled her *week.* So he gave him his daughter Rachel as wife also."

It's clear that, in this context, "week" is a Hebrew idiom for a period of seven years. In fact, we see the same exact language just a couple of chapters later. In Gen. 31:40-42, Jacob is arguing with Laban, and he exclaims: "There I was! In the day the drought consumed me, and the frost by night, and my sleep departed from my eyes. Thus I have been in your house twenty years; I served you *fourteen years for your two daughters,* and six years for your flock" (emphasis mine).

All right, we've established that Daniel's "week" (or "seven") is a reference to a seven-year period. Now go back to Daniel 9, and let's look again at the first half of v. 27: "Then he shall confirm a covenant with many for one week; but in the middle of the week he shall bring an end to sacrifice and offering." How many days are there in a week? Seven. What's half of seven? Three and a half. This verse says that at the midpoint of this "week" the man who brokered the covenant will somehow violate the treaty by "bringing an end to sacrifice and offering."

Now we have to ask another question or two here. First, who is the "many" with whom the Antichrist makes this pact? Well, it has to include the people who make sacrifices and offerings. How do we know that? Because it's obvious that this man's way of breaking the treaty is by going in and sabotaging this group's religious practices.

Are there any guesses as to who this could be? It must be someone who makes sacrifices and offerings, and the only people who do that to the one true God is *Israel*. But that's not all we can get out of this. Second, we should ask, "How can anyone stop Israel's sacrifices, since they aren't doing any?" That's easy; they can't! The only way that Israel can be *stopped* from making sacrifices is if they're *making* sacrifices! This must necessarily point to a future time, a time when Israel will have a temple in operation again.

Here's another question: How do we know that this must happen in the future? Because no one has ever made a seven-year treaty with anyone and then violated the treaty's terms by disrupting their worship of the Lord halfway through that treaty. So what we see, just in the first half of Dan. 9:27, is that "someone" (Antichrist) will bring peace through a treaty with Israel that's supposed to last seven years. Israel will be allowed to worship their God by putting their temple back into operation. This also means that we need to be keeping our ears to the ground, waiting to hear the Jewish people start clamoring for a rebuilt temple!

I want to talk for a minute about the rebuilding of the temple. Keep in mind that we're making a case for the fifth end-time prophecy, that Israel will be *safe* in her land. I would daresay that if Israel is at any point allowed to reconstruct her temple, it's going to have to be under conditions that are very different from what they are experiencing today. For one thing, the Temple Mount is presently occupied by a different religious group; the Muslims have placed there the third most important site in Islam, the Dome of the Rock. But the Temple Mount also is currently home to another significant piece of architecture. Do you remember what that is? Turn to the Olivet Discourse, Matthew 24. Chapters 24 and 25 comprise Jesus' longest monologue on the things of the end. Let's see what kicks off this lengthy sermon; read Matt. 24:1-2. Jesus is shown the temple complex by His disciples, and in v. 2 he says that every last stone would be thrown down. The question I want to ask here is, "Has that happened yet?" Now we're getting into a big concept, what's known as the "Law of Double Fulfillment." This is a theological term that is used to describe a prophecy in the Bible that is fulfilled once in part, and then once in full later on. (We'll experience this idea again when we start in on the Antichrist.)

This is actually a marvelous example of this law. Jesus clearly predicted that every single stone of the temple complex would be thrown down. In A.D. 70, that <u>mostly</u> happened, but not entirely. In fact, the "not entirely" part of the temple still stands today, on the Temple Mount! I'm speaking, of course, of the "Western Wall," or what's often referred to as the "Wailing Wall." We already know that the temple will at some point have to be rebuilt. We also know that the temple will have to be <u>completely</u> destroyed. It seems perfectly logical that the temple will be rebuilt to fulfill one part of the prophecy, and then it will be destroyed in its entirety in order to fulfill the other part.

Because Israel will one day be at peace with her neighbors prior to being attacked, and because she will have enough clout to do something so bizarre and unthinkable as to actually build and operate an Old Testament style of temple in the presence of her enemies, that can only mean that someone with great charisma and skill must come along and make these things happen. Enter Antichrist, the "Prince of False Peace."

That brings us to the first judgment of God, the "first seal" of the Tribulation period. So turn to the end of your Bible, and find Revelation 6. This chapter introduces us to the seven seals. The seal judgments, as they are sometimes called, are the first in a series of three sets of judgments, with seven judgments in each series. We will look at the other judgments later on, during our examination of the Tribulation. But let's look at the first seal, which is found in vs. 1-2: "Now I saw when the Lamb opened one of the seals; and I heard one of the four living creatures saying with a voice like thunder, 'Come and see.' And I looked, and behold, a white horse. He who sat on it had a bow; and a crown was given to him, and he went out conquering and to conquer."

This judgment is the unveiling of the man called "Antichrist." Verse 2 speaks of a white horse, which is symbolic of peace. I say this for two reasons. Reason number one is the first four seals are represented by horses of a different color. Read v. 4. The second seal is the red horse of war. Now read vs. 5-6. Here is a black horse, which is associated with famine. Finally, read v. 8. This fourth seal is the pale horse of death.

Each of these horses represents a different judgment, and each judgment is tied to the color of its corresponding horse. Second, notice that v. 4 says that peace will be taken from the earth. Peace can only be taken if peace is what currently prevails. All we have to do is use basic deductive reasoning to figure out that if the second seal is the removal of peace, then the first seal has to mean that it's creating the presence of peace.

So the rider of the white horse is going to bring peace. Please notice also, in v. 2, that this man on the white horse had a bow and was given a crown. The bow is symbolic of war, but there are no arrows. The Antichrist will wield a Gatling gun, but the weapon will have no ammunition. He'll have silos, but the missiles will have been removed. This would imply that he will rise to power under the specter of violence, but ultimately without bloodshed.

This is entirely consistent with what is described by Daniel's prophecy; he will become the first potentate to rule the entire world, and he will achieve it by using intrigue and political maneuvering rather than through military aggression. The fact that his crown was given to him indicates that his ascendency to the throne will likewise be peaceable; it will be freely given to him by acclamation from the whole world. No one will oppose him; none will raise their hand against him in his rapid trajectory to the highest position in all of history.

The Antichrist, then, is going to bring peace, albeit a very brief period of peace, which is how he'll come to power. In the same way that this peace will be followed by all-out war, the wave of peace that Antichrist will ride to world domination must also come from a time of global unrest. Think of it this way. If a man were to go about the task of taking over the whole world, and if he was able to do it by bringing peace to the world, then it stands to reason that he must bring peace when there is no peace. In other words, the only way this man is going to impress the world is by bringing something to the table that the world lacks but craves at any price.

For a brief explanation of this idea, turn back to Matthew 24 and read vs. 3-8. Jesus says that the "beginning of sorrows," or "birth pains" — which is a reference to the onset of the Tribulation — will be characterized by things like worldwide chaos and upheaval.

To summarize this fifth observation of end-time prophecy, I'm constantly on the lookout for two things: the people of the world clamoring for peace at all costs, and the Jewish people demanding to get their temple back. There has been a crescendo of voices over the past several years that are beginning to sing a single hymn in unison, a demand for world peace. Now, in just the past year or so, there is a chorus in the background that's been added to that hymn. We're starting to hear from the Jewish people who want to take up their sacrifices of temple worship once more.

Here's a quick review. There are five things so far that I've shown you that tell us we're in the last days. We're running around like headless chickens and acquiring knowledge at blinding speed. Israel is "back from the grave" and is once again its own sovereign nation. The Roman Empire is rising out of the ashes. A multinational coalition of forces (notables include Russia, Iran and Turkey) are lining up to destroy Israel. The world is screaming for peace while the Jews are preparing to make a pitch for a rebuilt temple. Now let's turn our attention away from Israel for the time being. I want to show you a couple more major signs that tell us we're in the final hours of the Church Age.

Chapter 4

Two More Signs

As if we didn't have enough to go on already, I want to give a sixth and seventh reason for us to know that we are perched near the end of God's "end time graph." Consider the words of the apostle Paul: "But know this, that in the last days perilous times will come: For men will be lovers of themselves, lovers of money, boasters, proud, blasphemers, disobedient to parents, unthankful, unholy, unloving, unforgiving, slanderers, without self-control, brutal, despisers of good, traitors, headstrong, haughty, lovers of pleasure rather than lovers of God, having a form of godliness but denying its power" (II Tim. 3:1-5).

Honestly, I don't see a need to elaborate on this very much. I know that some will say that these verses could describe many eras throughout the course of history. But I have a two-fold reply to that. In the first place, this has to be a worldwide situation the scriptures are describing, which we are seeing now but never have seen before. In the second place, to write this passage off by declaring that this could describe any period in history is to render God's Word here totally meaningless. It *must* refer to a specific time in history, or there would be no need for God to tell us these things.

Let's look at one last prophecy, one last thing, which tells us we can know that the last days are truly upon us. Again, we hear from Paul: "Now, brethren, concerning the coming of our Lord Jesus Christ and our gathering together to Him, we ask you, not to be soon shaken in mind or troubled, either by spirit or by word or by letter, as if from us, as though the day of Christ had come. Let no one deceive you by any means; for that Day will not come unless the falling away comes first, and the man of sin is revealed, the son of perdition, who opposes and exalts himself above all that is called God or that is worshiped, so that he sits as God in the temple of God, showing himself that he is God" (II Thess. 2:1-4). We're not going to spend a lot of time on this passage right now because it's something we're going to revisit in greater detail when we get to my exposition of the Antichrist. So let's fly through this, shall we?

Verse 1 introduces us to Paul's recurring theme of the Rapture, as he tells the people of Thessalonica that he wants to briefly discuss the matter of the "coming of our Lord Jesus Christ and *our gathering together to Him...*" That is surely a reference to the Rapture, which is worded similarly to the consummate passage on the subject in I Thess. 4:13-17. Then v. 2 says that the people don't need to fret over the erroneous belief that they somehow missed the Rapture and are now stuck in the Tribulation.

It's this next verse, v. 3, that I want to camp on for a moment. Paul says here that the Day of the Lord (another name for the Tribulation) won't come until two things happen, and the Greek text puts them in rapid succession. Those two things are the "falling away" and the revealing of "the man of sin." We have looked at half a dozen things Paul could easily have chosen to mention that we should be on the lookout for when it comes to the end of the age. But God gave Paul something else instead; He told Paul to warn us of the "falling away." Some people have said that this phrase could be translated as a "departure," which might be another way of saying "Rapture." I must hasten to reply that it's my belief that this is a use of linguistics in a highly suspect manner.

The word for "falling away" here, in the Greek, is "apostasia". It means "defection; revolt; apostasy, forsake." Paul already spoke of the Rapture in v. 1, using different terminology, and he never used the word "apostasia" in any of his epistles to describe anything about the Rapture whatsoever. All the evidence, then, points to a specific event that is not the Rapture, but it must take place in connection with the timing of the Rapture.

What, then, is Paul saying here? It's been well said that if the plain sense makes good sense, then it makes no sense to seek any other sense lest it become nonsense. This "apostasy," or rebellion, can only mean that people in droves, probably all over the world, will turn their backs on things they had previously held dear. I once thought that this would be limited to Christians, but it appears to be such a universal prediction by Paul that it might extend to all kinds of people from every imaginable type of religious (or even nonreligious) background. At this very moment, there are millions of Americans who are giving up on the greatness of our country and how God had made us great. Whether they're questioning the methods we use to vote (our Electoral College, for instance, is rapidly falling into disrepute) or they're revolting against the godly heritage of our country's founders, people all over the U.S. are rejecting, or "apostatizing," the American way.

Roman Catholics are pushing back against long-held Catholic traditions. There are the unruly "Nuns on the Bus," a group of left-leaning nuns who are fighting for causes of so-called "social justice."[1] High-ranking government officials who claim to be Catholic are openly rebelling against Catholic dogma on things like abortion and divorce. Even the popes are getting in on the act. Benedict recently resigned his post rather than wait until he died, something that hasn't happened in more than 500 years.[2] And Francis, Benedict's successor, has refused to condemn homosexuality.[3] He's even said that atheists can go to heaven![4]

In short, the world has been turned upside down. People no longer believe the things they once did. If Paul is going to bypass monumental things like the rebirth of the Jewish State and the resuscitation of Rome and instead select something he calls a "falling away," one can only assume that whatever is meant by that term, it must refer to something really, really BIG. I believe that the falling away refers to an apostasy, or rebellion, against virtually everything that people all over the world had once believed for hundreds of years. I also think that that's a vivid picture of where we are now.

If I may, I'd like to give you an example of how the church is falling away. We've nibbled at the corners of it a little bit, but let's look more directly at this subject with some Scripture to back us up. We've mentioned that there seems to be a growing number of people, even church members, who are beginning to downplay the fact that Jesus is returning. But I want to ask you to read some passages from the New Testament that have something to say about the Second Coming. It's a bit of a lengthy list, but it helps illustrate my point. Read these verses: Matt. 26:62-66; Mark 13:24-27; Luke 17:28-30; 21:25-28; Acts 1:9-11; I Cor. 1:7-8; 11:23-26; Phil. 3:20; Col. 3:1-4; II Thess. 1:6-7; Tit. 2:11-13; I John 2:28; Jude 14-15; Rev. 1:7; 22:20-21.

What I'm about to say, I want to say in all seriousness. Anyone who says that our Lord Jesus isn't returning bodily to this earth is guilty of at least heresy and probably even out-and-out blasphemy. Twenty-three of the twenty-seven books of the New Testament make at least one mention of His Second Coming, and one out of every 25 verses in the New Testament addresses the subject. The Second Coming of our Lord is beyond question one of the most important themes in Scripture. But the Bible warned us that the time would come when people would embrace and teach the wicked lie that He isn't coming back.

Consider the words of Peter: "Beloved, I now write to you this second epistle (in both of which I stir up your pure minds by way of reminder), that you may be mindful of the words which were spoken before by the holy prophets, and of the commandment of us, the apostles of the Lord and Savior, knowing this first: that scoffers will come in the last days, walking according to their own lusts, and saying, 'Where is the promise of His coming? For since the fathers fell asleep, all things continue as they were from the beginning of creation.' For this they willfully forget: that by the word of God the heavens were of old, and the earth standing out of water and in the water, by which the world that then existed perished, being flooded with water. But the heavens and the earth which are now preserved by the same word, are reserved for fire until the day of judgment and perdition of ungodly men" (II Pet. 3:1-7). Peter says these scoffers will deny things like special creation, catastrophes (such as the Flood), the Second Coming, and the judgment and destruction of the world.

Well, that makes seven different prophetic clues that tell us we're in the end times. Our frenzied lifestyles, the return of national Israel, the revival of Rome, the strange bedfellows coming together against Israel, the world looking for peace while Israel considers a rebuilt temple, the danger and savagery of our times, and the "falling away" all combine to make a strong case that we're about to see the end of the age. I would now like to turn your attention to the second part of this book; let's look at the coming Rapture.

Part Two

The Rapture of the Church

Chapter 5

Introduction to the "Catching Away"

Read Matt. 16:1-3. Jesus said the Pharisees and Sadducees could only read signs from an earthly perspective. His charge against them was that they couldn't perceive things from a heavenly viewpoint. And because they couldn't, He called them "hypocrites."

Now read Luke 12:54-56. Here, Jesus was speaking to a larger crowd, and He accused them of the same kind of thing, that they could understand temporary and less important things like weather, but they couldn't see the signs of the times. And again, He calls them "hypocrites." Why? Because they're worried about the temporary things of this world instead of the weightier things of eternity, yet they had counted themselves as being God's people. But God's people consistently strive to see things God's way.

Jesus said that no one knows the day or hour of His return, but some people get carried away and interpret that to mean that we can't know *anything* about when He might come back. That's letting the pendulum swing too far the other way. Remember the words of Heb. 10:24-25, which I quoted on the title page to this book. God expects us to see His judgment coming (i.e. the "Day approaching"), and if we can't see the signs around us, He says we're *hypocrites*.

We just saw, in Part One, seven excellent reasons that we can know for sure that we're living in the lengthening shadows of the very end of the Church Age. As a result, I'm not going to take up any more ink trying to prove my case on this point. Nor am I going to try and prove a case for a coming Rapture. There are five prevailing views on when the Rapture of the church is going to occur in relation to the Tribulation, and we will look at each of them. As we go through this section, I anticipate that it will become self-evident to everyone that there will indeed be a catching away of God's people, irrespective of when it is to take place relative to the Tribulation.

There are several instances in Scripture where someone was carried alive into heaven, and I want to ask you to read each of these passages in order that you might become familiar with these occurrences. That way, when you get to the verses that describe the Rapture of the entire body of Christ, you will have already gotten your feet wet to this doctrine. There are many Christians today who don't believe in a coming Rapture. It is my prayer that, once you have read this section, you won't be counted among them.

Please read the following: Gen. 5:21-24; II Kgs. 2:9-12; Acts 1:9-11; II Cor. 12:2-4; Heb. 11:5; Rev. 4:1-2; 11:7-12. Each of these passages describes the sudden translation of individual persons (or, in the case of the witnesses in Revelation 11, two persons) from earth into heaven. Please notice that the verse in Hebrews leaves no doubt that Enoch, the man who "walked with God" in Genesis 5, was truly raptured, carried away without ever having tasted death. In II Kings, Elijah enjoyed the same experience as Enoch in that he never died. Paul (in II Corinthians) and John (Revelation) both died, but not before they were given a glimpse of heaven while still in their mortal bodies. In Acts, Jesus was "raptured" in what had to be one of the most amazing and glorious events in all of history, the Ascension.

With all of these case precedents, it should come as no surprise to anyone that there's coming a day when ALL believers, both the quick and the dead, will be taken in like manner to be with our Lord. Having these thoughts in mind, let's begin by looking at the Rapture view known as "Pretribulationism." We'll follow that with a look at Posttribulationism, Midtribulationism, the "Partial Rapture" theory, and the "Pre-Wrath" theory.

Chapter 6

Pretribulationism

This view teaches that Jesus will come to rapture the church prior to the beginning of the Tribulation. One reason for this view is because wherever the Tribulation is mentioned in the Bible, Israel is always mentioned but the church never is. For examples of this, read the following passages: Deut. 4:27-31; Jer. 30:4-11; Matt. 24:15-31; Rev. 4-18. One of the main reasons we'll be raptured before the Tribulation is because God didn't appoint us to wrath (cf. Rom. 5:9; I Thess. 1:9-10; 5:9-10).

There are a number of instances where God spared His elect before judgment fell. As you saw above, Enoch (Gen. 5:24) was raptured just before the Flood. Lot was taken out of Sodom before judgment came to that wicked city (Genesis 19). In Genesis 6, Noah and his family were kept out of harm's way during the Flood. It's been argued by opponents of the pretribulational view that Noah had to go through the Flood, but the response to that is really very easy. *Someone* had to go through this judgment in order to repopulate the earth, and besides, at no time was Noah's family ever in mortal danger. There was a zero percent chance that they would fail to make it through the deluge, since that was God's plan and Noah was obedient in following the Lord's instructions.

In the case of the plagues of Egypt, the children of Israel were protected from harm. In Joshua 6, Rahab's family was protected from destruction because of her willingness to help Israel in Joshua's campaign against Jericho. There are plenty more examples throughout Scripture that we can point to, but it's clear that there is a recurring theme running through the Bible that shows us how God keeps His people protected from the wrath He unleashes on the rebellious masses.

In order to lay a foundation for discussing the Rapture, it's only fitting that we take a quick look at the primary passages that describe the event. There are three notable passages in the New Testament that deal with the Rapture, and I'd like you to read them in succession. Read I Cor. 15:50-53; I Thess. 4:13-17; Rev. 4:1-2. There are several words, phrases and concepts that these verses hold in common, which help us see this blessed event with greater clarity. One such word that jumps out at us is the word "trumpet." Have you ever heard anyone say that they're listening for the sound of a trumpet to call them home? This is where that idea comes from. The voice that sounded like a trumpet, calling John up to heaven, is the voice we'll also hear that will carry us home.

Let's talk about the book of Revelation for a minute, just to start getting familiar with it. It's the most organized of any of the books of the Bible. Follow along as I give you its outline, and you'll see what I mean. Chapter 1 is the introduction to the book. Chapters 2-3 are letters to the seven churches. Seven being the number of completeness, these letters represent the entire church age. Chapter 4 opens with the rapture of John, which is followed by a picture of worship in heaven throughout chapters 4-5.

Chapters 6-19 cover the Tribulation, with the end of chapter 19 ending in the "Parousia," or Second Coming of the Lord. Chapter 20 is the Millennium, the destruction of Satan in the lake of fire, and the Great White Throne judgment (the judgment of all the lost people throughout history). Chapters 21-22 describe the new heaven and earth. It's worthy of mention that the church is not discussed anywhere in Revelation after the end of Chapter 3, the close of the church age. (There is one mention of the church in Rev. 22:16, but it is simply a summary statement reminding John that this letter is a testimony to be circulated among the churches.) The fact that John is raptured just prior to the beginning of the Tribulation speaks volumes about where we as the body of Christ can expect to be once the judgment of God begins, particularly if we give credence to the fact that the church is not mentioned one single time in the chapters that deal with the Tribulation.

That's the book of Revelation in a nutshell. Now go back and read Rev. 3:10. At first glance, one might say that this is a statement to the church at Philadelphia in the first century. However, that's impossible, because Jesus says He'll keep His faithful church from the hour of trial "which shall come upon the whole world." That time has not come, so obviously the Lord had an intended audience other than the first-century church of Philadelphia.

But I'm not done with this verse. Look at the phrase at the end, where it says that this coming trial is designed to test those "...who dwell on the earth." That phrase is found in several other places in Revelation; read 6:10; 8:13; 11:9-10; 13:8, 14; 17:8. Revelation consistently uses this oft-repeated refrain to refer to people who reject God. Remember that we, as Christians, are citizens of heaven (Phil. 3:20). Those who love the things of this world are enemies of God (Jas. 4:4), and as such these "earth-dwellers" are the people left behind after the Rapture to be judged by seven years of hell on earth.

Now I want to take a look at the "Restrainer." Read II Thess. 2:1-10. In v. 1, Jesus comes and gathers us to Him; this is a direct reference to the Rapture. Verse 2 addresses the people of Thessalonica that were afraid that they'd missed the Rapture and the Tribulation had begun. In vs. 3-4, Paul explains that a "falling away," or "rebellion," must precede the coming of the Antichrist.

Next, read vs. 6-8: "And now you know what is restraining, that he may be revealed in his own time. For the mystery of lawlessness is already at work; only He who now restrains will do so until He is taken out of the way. And then the lawless one will be revealed, whom the Lord will consume with the breath of His mouth and destroy with the brightness of His coming."

This Restrainer, who is described as a "He" rather than an "it," must be more powerful than Satan. We know this because the devil is being prevented from doing a specific diabolical deed as long as this restraining presence is exercising influence on the earth. Ultimately, this Restrainer will be "taken out of the way" in order that the Antichrist (the "lawless one") will be able to come to power. Just back up a few verses and read vs. 3-4 again, and then read vs. 8-10.

I see only one possibility for the identity of the "Restrainer," and that would be none other than the Holy Spirit of God. Only God is more powerful than Satan! Taken as a whole, this passage tells us that the Holy Spirit (the Restrainer) must be taken out of the way (a reference to the Rapture), and *then* the devil can unleash the Antichrist. Understood properly, this can only mean that the Rapture must occur before the Tribulation can begin, especially since the revealing of Antichrist is what sets off the Tribulation itself. We will discuss this at greater length when we get to the Tribulation period in Part Three.

Another reason for the Pretribulational view of the Rapture is because of the analogy of the Jewish wedding. According to Matt. 9:15, Jesus is the groom, whereas the church is His bride (Eph. 5:22-32; Rev. 19:7). There are three parts to a Jewish wedding. First, the marriage is enacted by the parents of the bride and groom. Second, the groom is to build on a room to the father's house. And third, the groom comes for his bride at an unannounced time, where he carries her off to the father's house. Once there, family and friends attend the wedding and celebrate with a feast that usually lasts for several days.

Compare this scenario with our relationship to Jesus. First, God saves us, which makes us a part of the bride (i.e. the church). The next thing to come will be the Rapture. This is where Jesus will come and take us to the Father's house, as He has prepared a place for us there (John 14:1-3). The marriage of the Groom to His bride will take place in heaven (Rev. 19:6-8). Finally comes the marriage supper (Luke 22:14-18, 28-30).

All right, let's shift gears just a little bit. Go back and read I Thess. 4:13-17 again, only this time keep reading down through v. 18. If these words are to be of comfort, how comforting would it be to hear that you're going to get roughed up in the Tribulation before you're raptured? (I'll expand on this thought again a little later.) By the way, here's one good way to know that we're not in the Tribulation right now: there are still places in the world where it's dangerous to be a Christian (just like there always have been), but there are also safe places. During the Tribulation, there will be <u>no</u> safe place to be a Christian.

I want to finish this chapter with one last pitch for the pretribulational rapture. This is highly significant. I want to argue that the Rapture is an event that is always and forever an "imminent" event. What does that mean? Simply put, it means that it is something that can happen at any time. Pretribulationism contends that the Rapture can occur at any moment, which doesn't fit with any of the other theories. Look at Rom. 13:11-12: "And do this, knowing the time, that now it is high time to awake out of sleep; for now our salvation is nearer than when we first believed. The night is far spent, the day is at hand. Therefore let us cast off the works of darkness, and let us put on the armor of light." Salvation is described here as a future event, much like the wording that you find in I Cor. 1:18 ("For the message of the cross is foolishness to those who are perishing, but to us who are being saved it is the power of God").

The future tense description of our salvation means that this carries with it an eschatological meaning. Read Phil. 3:20; Tit. 2:11-13. We're eagerly awaiting the coming of the Lord; we use the word "eagerly" because He could come at any moment. Jas. 5:7-9 explains the concept this way: "Therefore be patient, brethren, until the coming of the Lord. See how the farmer waits for the precious fruit of the earth, waiting patiently for it until it receives the early and latter rain. You also be patient. Establish your hearts, for the coming of the Lord is at hand. Do not grumble against one another, brethren, lest you be condemned. Behold, the Judge is standing at the door!"

He is standing at the door, but no one knows when that door will fly open! If the Rapture could occur at any moment, without our knowing when, none of the other theories can work (which is what I shall explain to you over the next several chapters). This is the case for the pretribulational Rapture. Now turn the page, and we'll begin an examination of the Posttribulational position.

Chapter 7

Posttribulationism

As we go through these views on the timing of the Rapture, there are a number of scripture references that we will be looking at again and again. One such passage is the verse I want to go back to now, and that is Rev. 3:10. As you read this verse again, I want to ask you to think as the Posttribulationist would think. The "Posttribber" would say that, according to passages like this one, the Bible teaches that believers will be saved *through* the Tribulation rather than being taken *out* of it. What we discussed about this verse back in Chapter 6 should adequately refute this interpretation.

Now read Rev. 20:4-6. The posttribulational view teaches that this is a description of all believers being resurrected (or raptured) at the end of the Tribulation. By contrast, the pretribulational position says that these verses are talking about the people who get saved and martyred during the Tribulation. We know that many will be saved during the Tribulation, as that is the function of the 144,000 young Jewish men described in Revelation 7 and the two witnesses of Chapter 11 (whom we shall discuss in greater detail in Part Three).

I start to run into immediate trouble, though, when I take a step back and look at this view in its entirety. Two big problems leap out at me. First, Jesus says that no one can know the day or the hour when He will return (cf. Mark 13:32-37). (This is that subject of "imminence" again, which we covered in the previous chapter.) The Lord tells us plainly that we can't know the exact time of His return, so Posttribulationism is untenable because we would know precisely when the Second Coming will take place. It will be, down to the day, exactly seven years after the Antichrist signs the treaty between Israel and the world (Dan. 9:27). And second, the posttribulational view cannot explain who will populate the millennial kingdom in their mortal bodies.

This sounds perhaps a little bit complicated, but it's really not. Read Isa. 65:20-23. During the Millennium, there will be mortals who will marry, produce children, grow old, and die. If all believers are raptured at the Second Coming, then no believers will be left in their mortal bodies (I Cor. 15:50-54). The Bible teaches that there will be both glorified believers and mortal saved people (the former coming from the Church Age, the latter from the Tribulation) that will enter into the Millennium. Again, the pretribulational position is able to pass the test of reconciling the whole counsel of God, whereas the other views on the Rapture are ultimately and invariably left wanting.

Chapter 8

Midtribulationism

This view takes us back to Revelation. Go back there and read 11:3-12. The midtribulational belief states that the two witnesses are representative of the church. They say that we're saved from God's "wrath," which begins at the midpoint of the Tribulation. I need to interject that at the halfway point of the Tribulation, i.e. 3-1/2 years into it, there are several major cataclysms that occur and usher in the final 3-1/2 years, what's frequently called the "Great Tribulation."

If the midtribulational view is correct that the church is represented by these two witnesses, then the church will be able to kill people by breathing fire on them, we will keep rain from falling on the earth throughout our 42-month ministry, we'll turn water into blood, we'll all be confined to the city of Jerusalem, and we'll all die at the same time and then be collectively resurrected and raptured 3-1/2 days later.

Midtribulationism says that the Rapture occurs at the "last trumpet" (I Cor. 15:52). In Rev. 11:15, the seventh trumpet judgment begins. This system of belief argues that this is at the midpoint of the Tribulation (although I've not heard anyone ever successfully defend that scripturally), so this "last trumpet" is simultaneously representative of both the final trumpet judgment and the Rapture. However, the Pretribulationalist would counter that the trumpets of judgment and the Rapture are unrelated. (See Lev. 23:23-25 for a ceremonial blowing of trumpets that has nothing to do with judgment.)

In order for this position to be right, the first half of the Tribulation cannot be part of God's "wrath." We will consider the ramifications of that argument when we get to Chapter 10. But just as it is with the posttribulational belief, Midtribulationism likewise teaches that Jesus will return at a specific appointed time. As a result, both of these views suffer from the same fatal flaw that *we cannot know the day or the hour of Jesus' return.*

Chapter 9

Partial Rapture

This theory has nothing to do with the timing of the Rapture, and instead only concerns itself with the *quantity* and *quality* of Christians that will be taken out of this world when Jesus comes for His church. Those who adhere to this doctrine would argue that only <u>some</u> believers will be raptured. They get this idea from two primary sources. First, there's II Tim. 4:8, where Paul writes: "Finally there is laid up for me the crown of righteousness, which the Lord, the righteous Judge, will give to me on that Day, and not to me only but also to all who have loved His appearing." The other passage, which is worded similarly, is Heb. 9:27-28: "And as it is appointed for men to die once, but after this the judgment, so Christ was offered once to bear the sins of many. To those who eagerly wait for Him He will appear a second time, apart from sin, for salvation."

The suggestion here is that only the "faithful" and "watchful" Christians who are eagerly looking for Him to appear will be raptured. This is sort of like a "Protestant Purgatory" (to coin a term); if you're not good enough, you'll have to go through the Tribulation in order to be purified. This belief is full of holes, but I'll give you the three main ones that come to mind. In the first place, that's not fair to those who are alive at the time of the Rapture and have to go through the

Tribulation, whereas those who already died saved but wouldn't have been "good enough" were spared the time of Jacob's Trouble because they were fortunate enough to have died beforehand.

Second, this belief plants seeds of doubt that God never intended for us to have. It forces us to ask ourselves questions like "How faithful is faithful enough?" "How watchful is watchful enough?" "How eager is eager enough?" This comes dangerously close to a salvation based on works, a false gospel that condemns rather than saves! We must never forget that one of the pillars of the gospel is that the focus is on the perfect righteousness of Jesus and not on ourselves. Either Jesus' death was satisfactory to save completely or it wasn't satisfactory to save at all. There is no middle ground here, but that's exactly what this view tries to force into the outer edges of the Good News.

Third, go back and read I Thess. 4:13-18 again. The first five verses describe the Rapture, and then Paul gives the admonition in v. 18 to "...comfort one another with these words." This causes us to ask even more questions, doesn't it? I mean, how comforting would these words be? Stop and think about it. Imagine how encouraging it would be for Paul to tell his hearers something like this: "Hey, everybody! I have good news! For those of you who are good enough to make the cut, there's a 'Get out of the Tribulation free' card. The rest of you that are saved but not good enough, well, you'll have to stick around and see if you can survive seven years of hell on earth. Oh, by the way, I don't know how good is good enough, so we'll all just have to wait and find out when the Rapture happens. And oh, yeah, I also don't know how to distinguish between the unsaved and the 'saved but not good enough for the Rapture' categories, so some of you might be getting left behind because you're not good enough Christians while others of you will be left because you're not Christians at all. But I don't have any idea who fits into what category, and I can't give you any advice on how you can know for yourselves, either. So cheer up and be comforted!"

If you don't know whether or not you're good enough to go in the Rapture, how can you know you're good enough to go to heaven at all? Does the Bible really teach that you can know you have eternal life (cf. I John 5:13), but that you can't know if you're good enough to be raptured? While I disagree with all the theories on the Rapture save the pretribulational view, the others have at least a morsel of biblical merit and are therefore not classifiable as heresy. The Partial Rapture theory, however, is both heretical and dangerous. It cannot be taken seriously as a doctrine worthy of even the slightest consideration.

how did these martyrs get saved? I have two possible answers. First, and the more obvious solution, is that the two witnesses of Revelation 11 will bring in a harvest. (Again, we'll explore these two characters at length in due course.)

Second, consider Gen. 4:25-26: "And Adam knew his wife again, and she bore a son and named him Seth, 'For God has appointed another seed for me instead of Abel, whom Cain killed.' And as for Seth, to him also a son was born; and he named him Enosh. Then men began to call on the name of the Lord." These men, who lived on history's earliest pages, began to call on the name of the Lord with no explanation given to us. It seems more than reasonable that the same thing could happen again with these people at the far end of time yet future. These people will by no means be without testimony. Many will have heard warnings from Christians before the church was taken up, warnings about the Rapture itself. There will be those who've heard about the Savior, and still others will have the silent but beckoning Word of God, that precious Word for which so many saints have died in order that it might be preserved.

Now as to this business about the phrase that tells us God's wrath "has come," read Rev. 6:17. Here we see that the day of God's wrath has now come, the argument by the Pre-Wrath view being that this is the beginning of God's wrath. The proponents of this view say that everything up to this point has *not* been God's wrath. But in Rev. 11:18, after the seventh trumpet judgment, the 24 elders around the throne of God announce that His wrath "has come." Furthermore, in Rev. 14:6-7, also after that seventh and final trumpet judgment, an angel comes down from heaven and says that the hour of God's judgment "has come." That's the exact same phrase in the Greek that's used by the ungodly in Revelation 6. If we have to be here for the seal judgments because God's wrath hasn't come until they're nearly finished, who's to say that we won't have to stay through the trumpet judgments, too?

As I commented at the beginning of this chapter, the burden of proof with the Pre-Wrath camp lies in the first six seal judgments. If there is to be any chance that this doctrine is correct, those who hold to this view must be able to show that these judgments are not part of God's wrath. (This is only logical, since they call it the "Pre-Wrath" theory.) This is where their entire system breaks down.

Let's begin the deconstruction by reviewing the word "wrath." Read Rev. 6:8. This verse says that the first four seals will be the cause of the death of 25% of the world's population. To my mind, that <u>must</u> be categorized as being "wrathful" on God's part. But I don't want to just give you my opinion; I need to back up this statement with Scripture. Read Rom. 1:20-28. This is a picture of God giving a people up to their own vile passions and simply allowing them to do what their evil natures desire. Now go back and read the preamble to this section; read v. 18. God reveals His wrath simply by taking His hand off of a nation or people. In other words, the argument that seals one through six aren't part of God's wrath doesn't hold water.

The reason the Bible can still say that God's people aren't appointed to God's wrath is that even though

God has judged and is now judging many peoples (including the U.S.), He hasn't done it on a global scale since the Flood. When God removes His hand, and when the Restrainer is taken out, that will be the commencement of God's wrath upon the whole world. As my wife Debbie puts it, a child can be abused without his parents ever having to lay a hand on him.

To drive one final nail into the coffin of this theory, read Ezek. 5:11-13. The first four seals of the Tribulation are Antichrist, war, famine, and death. They're represented and described by the four horses.

In Ezek. 5:13, the NASB states that God will have His "wrath" satisfied when He puts Israel through His judgment, which includes famine, war, and death. These judgments are clearly defined here as being part of God's wrath, and they're completely identical to the judgments outlined in the first six seals. If famine, war, and death are part of God's "wrath" in the Old Testament, there is every reason to believe that they'll be part of God's wrath in the Tribulation as well.

This concludes our look at the Rapture and when it will happen in relation to the Tribulation. Let's move on to Part Three, and we'll begin our journey through the Tribulation itself.

Part Three

The Tribulation

Chapter 11

Why Will There Be a Tribulation?

The question must be asked: Why would God, who is the embodiment of love (I John 4:8, 16), subject His very own creation to the horrors of seven uninterrupted years of destruction and carnage? Before we attempt to answer this puzzler, I should interject that you and I live in a fallen world, corrupted by sin. We are clothed in fallen bodies, bodies that ache for sin, bodies that rush headlong into sin. And we have fallen minds, clouded by the pollution of sin. We do not and cannot have a perfect understanding of anything.

Consequently, when we ask why a "loving" God would do unimaginably awful things like those that characterize the coming Tribulation, we must take a step back and ask the prerequisite question: What does it mean when the Bible says that "God is love"? I do not have any chance, not in this lifetime anyway, of coming completely to grips with what God means when He says that He is love. I don't understand the way of the cross. The most basic thing in all of Christianity is the propitiatory death of Jesus by way of crucifixion, which is to say that He accomplished my salvation by taking my place. This transaction makes little sense to me. I do, however, *believe* it; I believe it with all I that I am and all that I have. I believe that

Jesus died to take away my sin, and in that death He took all of my sins upon Himself.

But it doesn't stop there. He also clothed me in His perfect righteousness. He took my sins, but then He gave me His perfection in the place of that sin. I now have the promise of being in the presence of the triune God for all eternity, and it's exclusively because the Son of God came and traded places with me. And can I be brutally honest with you for a moment? I truly do not understand this. I do believe it, and I praise God for it, but I cannot grasp it.

So if, in my sinful condition and limited mind, I am unable to plumb the depths of God's love for me, how can I completely answer the hard questions of God's ways in His dealings with the world? To put it simply, I can't, at least not completely and with 100% accuracy. But I would immediately add that God has both a right and a reasonable expectation that we can understand *enough* of what He says to us. What He communicates through His creation is clear, and His Word is clearer still. It is never proper for us to say that since we can't know anything perfectly, then we have the right to throw in the towel and simply give up on knowing anything at all. If that were the case, He would never have given us the Bible.

This topic of judgment and the Tribulation is foreign to most of us because it doesn't seem to fit the mold that we've been taught to put God into. But God does tell us these things, and therefore He exercises His right to insist that we try to comprehend them as best we're able. To that end, God expects that we can and should identify with these teachings to a reasonable degree, certainly a level that is far greater than for those who don't know the Savior.

To wrap up this thought, I'm going to give you several reasons why God is going to judge the world with such severity. This is not intended to be even close to an exhaustive list; it's designed to prompt your thinking, in order that you might see "the whole counsel of God" more clearly (Acts 20:27). We live in a day when it's increasingly unpopular to discuss such objectionable subjects as the judgment of God. But it's precisely because the world is unwilling to talk about these matters that you and I *must* discuss them with all the more urgency and openness. So fasten your seat belts, and let's prepare for a bumpy ride.

Why will there be a Tribulation? First, it's so God can cleanse the world. Read Gen. 6:5-13; I Pet. 3:18-20. His purpose for the Flood was to purge the world of sin and start with a clean slate. The reason for the Tribulation is the exact same thing.

Second, it's what the world wants. I know that may sound crazy, but read John 1:9-11; 3:16-19. Do you see what I mean? The world is *begging* to be judged. This flies directly in the face of the demonic doctrine that "man is basically good" and "God would never judge anybody." But God tells us through His Word that man is NOT good. Hence, God will undoubtedly judge the world one day, and when He does, it won't be pretty.

Third, to minimize God's judgment is to minimize the significance of the cross. If judgment is not going to be that bad, then Jesus died for nothing. If hell isn't exactly how the Bible presents it, as a real place where there will be eternal suffering for all who end up there, then Jesus' death was meaningless.

Fourth, God will use the Tribulation as the springboard to fulfill His promises to the patriarchs, namely the Abrahamic covenant. This covenant is introduced in Gen. 12:1-3, ratified in Gen. 15:18-21, reaffirmed in Gen. 17:1-21, and renewed to both Isaac (Gen. 26:2-5) and Jacob (Gen. 28:10-17). The covenant's ultimate fulfillment is unconditional and irrevocable (Jer. 31:31-37; Rom. 11). There are five parts to the covenant: (1) The people of Abraham (Gen. 17:2-7); (2) The land of Israel (Gen. 15:18-21; 17:8); (3) A nation (Gen. 12:2; 17:4); (4) Divine protection and blessing (Gen. 12:3); and (5) A king to rule them (II Sam. 7:8-16; Ps. 2:7-9; Isa. 9:6-7; Rev. 2:27; 11:15; 12:5; 19:11-16). God went to great lengths to explain this promise to the world, that there really is a future hope for the Jewish people (Jer. 29:11; Rom. 11:25-27; 15:8).[1]

The world hates God. As a result, the world hates God's people, both Jews and Christians. The world is lining up to destroy Israel because God made the aforementioned promises to her. Satan is instilling hatred for the Jews in the hearts of people and nations all over the world. A primary purpose of the Tribulation is for God to judge those who stumble over Jerusalem in order that He might clear the path for Israel to receive her King. Things are bad now, but they're only going to get worse. This world is on a one-way trip downward, and neither governments nor citizens will make them any better. Only Jesus can do that, and that's exactly what He'll do when He returns at the end of the Tribulation. Speaking of the Tribulation, let's talk about it. Here we go!

Chapter 12

A Time of Transition

So far, we've made a case for two things: we're indeed in the end times, and we'll be raptured home to heaven before the Tribulation begins. Now we shall turn our attention to the Tribulation, where we will examine some of the most important personalities and events of this seven-year time of testing that is to come upon the whole earth. Just as we asked in the foregoing chapter why there will even be a Tribulation, we could also reasonably ask the question why we would care about what happens in this dispensation if we're not going to be here for it. Let me give you a few reasons. First, it will be an encouragement to us as believers. We're experiencing enough bad stuff as it is. It should be comforting for us to know that we won't be here for the darkest days of all (I Thess. 4:18).

Second, it helps us see the signs leading up to the Tribulation and therefore we are able to see that we're getting even closer to the Rapture. (As Bible teacher David Jeremiah rightly says, prophetic events always cast a shadow before they happen.) Another reason we need to familiarize ourselves with the Tribulation is that it should motivate us to win the lost so they won't have to endure its horrors, either. In other words, knowing the gravity of the Tribulation should give us a sense of urgency to get out and evangelize our lost loved ones, knowing that our time may be very short.

Finally, it helps us get a hearing with the lost, as they can see the unfolding of prophecy, too. When our eschatology lines up with the Scriptures, we're able to explain world events with much greater accuracy and clarity than the secular news media ever could.

Over the next several chapters, I want to examine this time of judgment and sorrow. The first thing I want to do in this regard is make an observation about the Tribulation, that being how we know it will be so bad. I know of at least three forces at work that will combine to make this seven-year period the worst time in history: (1) The influence of the Holy Spirit, who presently indwells every believer alive on the earth, will be removed; (2) Satan will have a longer leash than at any time before; and (3) God Himself will be bringing judgment upon the earth.

To help us understand the seriousness and severity of these ingredients working together, let's look at what Paul has to say about it. For a little background, let's start with our old friend, I Thess. 4:13-18. We should all know what this is by now, a description of the Rapture itself. But let's start traveling into previously uncharted territory, the dark tunnels of the coming Day of the Lord. As you read these verses, don't stop at the end of Chapter 4. This time, keep reading and go down through 5:1-5. Notice how this section starts out. We just saw the Rapture, and the very next words (quoting the NKJV) are "But concerning the times and the seasons..." Those two words, "but concerning" (which the NASB more accurately translates "Now as to...") describe a transition within the same subject. Paul uses two tiny Greek words – "peri de" – several times in his letters to indicate a change of course under the same general subject. So he's telling us here in this passage that he's turning a slight corner but is still on the same road.

Notice that he makes a distinction between two kinds of people, the "you" and the "they." Let's read these verses again, and we'll put extra stress on the words "you" and "they." Here's the distinction Paul makes: <u>You</u> (1) have no need to be told; (2) have knowledge of the coming Day of the Lord; (3) are not in darkness; (4) shouldn't be surprised by the Day of the Lord; and (5) are sons of light and day, not of the night and darkness.

Now contrast that with Paul's description of the other group. <u>They</u> (1) proclaim "peace and safety"; (2) suffer sudden destruction; (3) will not escape. For a fun little exercise to do on your own, finish vs. 6-11 in the same way, and write down the differences between the "us" and the "them."

This is yet another case to be made for a pretribulational Rapture, especially since "they" will exclaim "peace and safety!" (which is what the Antichrist will promise the world), and then sudden destruction will take "them" by surprise. And this idea, the idea that all of lost humanity will be exhilarated by "peace at last" and then be swiftly plunged into chaos and destruction, leads us directly into the teeth of the first two judgments of the Tribulation.

This actually dovetails into where I want to go next, the book of Revelation and the horrors of the Tribulation itself. So let's turn there, to the very beginning of the last book of the Bible. While you're turning pages, let me explain a thing or two in just a little more detail.

I gave this chapter the title of "A Time of Transition" because there is a space of time between the Rapture and the beginning of the Tribulation. As we begin this section, keep in mind the fact that the Tribulation doesn't begin right after the Rapture. The Tribulation begins when the Antichrist signs a seven-year treaty with Israel (Dan. 9:26-27), so there are a few things that will have to happen before the treaty will be signed and God will start the seven-year countdown to Armageddon and the Second Coming.

Naturally, there will be the rise of Antichrist, which will not occur until after the Rapture. II Thess. 2:3 speaks of the coming "Day" (i.e. the Day of the Lord): "Let no one deceive you by any means; for that Day will not come unless the falling away comes first, and the man of sin is revealed, the son of perdition..." Once the Rapture takes place and God's people are removed from the earth in an instant, the restraining power of the Holy Spirit (II Thess. 2:5-8) will create an immediate vacuum where evil will take over the world in ways that no human can possibly fathom. The entire globe will be engulfed in chaos, confusion, and rampant wickedness. Someone will need to come in and fill that void, and that someone's name is "Antichrist." This evil man will come in and fill the void left by the Spirit of God when His restraining power, through His servants the Christians, are carried away from here and into heaven in the twinkling of an eye.

The Rapture will be a solitary and instantaneous event, but the things that follow won't be. I have heard several scholars refer to this period as a "time of preparation." Think of it as a sort of calm before the storm. We won't discuss much more about Antichrist until we get to Revelation 6, but I want to whet your appetite for our study of the Tribulation by helping you understand that the pieces of the puzzle have to start coming together along the way in order for some of the things we'll be reading about actually reach completion. I don't know how much time will elapse between the Rapture and the installation of Antichrist, and then how much longer it will take for him to sign that seven-year treaty, but my guess is that this "time of preparation" will last upwards of several months, maybe even half a year. Things will have to move fairly quickly, though, because without the glue of the church to hold this world together, everything is going to spiral rapidly out of control!

All right, find Revelation 1, and we'll begin our look at the Tribulation itself, as told through the apostle John. Take a deep breath, turn the page, and let's begin.

Chapter 13

When the Church Goes to Heaven

My goal here is to go through the Tribulation in chronological order, with the book of Revelation as our primary guide. Let's dive right in, and start with Chapter 1. Always keep in your mind the ultimate theme of this book, which is the *revealing* of the risen Jesus. Jesus was presented, a piece at a time, throughout the Old Testament. The gospels introduce Him as the Jewish Messiah. The epistles teach that He is Savior to both the Jew and the Gentile. Revelation is the icing on the cake, unveiling Him as the coming King of kings and Lord of lords.

Revelation has some seemingly confusing imagery in it, but don't be intimidated, as we shall soon discover how remarkably simple the plot is for us to follow. It starts with the statement of its purpose: "The Revelation of Jesus Christ, which God gave Him to show His servants – things which must shortly take place. And He sent and signified it by His angel to His servant John, who bore witness to the word of God, and to the testimony of Jesus Christ, to all things that he saw. Blessed is he who reads and those who hear the words of this prophecy, and keep those things which are written in it; for the time is near" (Rev. 1:1-3). Notice that the book's "mission statement" is given to us in the first five words, "The revelation of Jesus Christ." As long as we keep those five simple words in mind as we go through this, we'll always have an immovable reference point that will help keep us from getting lost.

There's another helpful tip here in this section we just read, and that's found in v. 3. It is essential for us to recognize that Revelation is the only book of the Bible that pronounces a blessing on those who read and keep its words. In fact, God is so serious about wanting us to understand and proclaim the truths in Revelation that He repeats the blessing again at the end, in 22:7: "Behold, I am coming quickly! Blessed is he who keeps the words of the prophecy of this book."

Moving on from here, Revelation also has a verse that gives the outline of the entire book. If we skip down and read 1:19, we read these words: "Write the things which you have seen, and the things which are, and the things which will take place after this." In this verse, Jesus tells John to write: (1) The things he was shown (the vision of the risen Lord in Chapter 1); (2) The things which are (the Church Age of Chapters 2 and 3); and (3) The things to come (the Rapture, Tribulation, Second Coming, Millennium, and eternity, all found in Chapters 4-22). As we make our way through Revelation, we'll see the clarity and simplicity of this little outline. All right, let's jump in and look at the first thing described, which are the things that John has seen.

Back up a few verses, and read 1:9-18. This is an introduction to the book, and it's a very interesting introduction because it's rare in Scripture that we're told that the author was writing specifically what God told him to write. The Old Testament prophets did that, but none of the other New Testament books give such statements. I don't know why that is, although it may be because of the controversy that this book has caused. Adrian Rogers used to say that the two books people fight over the most are Genesis and Revelation, and that's because Satan hates them the most. In Genesis, Satan's doom is prophesied, while in Revelation his doom is realized.

It's obvious from these verses that John is being visited by the King of kings, the risen and glorified Jesus. And in v. 11, the Lord tells John to write down everything he's about to be shown and then forward it to the seven churches of Asia. There is one little nugget of wisdom I'd like to extract from this verse (v. 11) before we move on. I always thought that Jesus wanted John to write seven letters separate from one another and then send each letter to the corresponding church.

You'll notice that 2:1 starts with the words: "To the angel of the church of Ephesus write..." Then, 2:8 says the same kind of thing: "And to the angel of the church in Smyrna write..."

This exact same set of words is used by the Lord to tell John what He wants said to each individual church, so I always assumed that John wrote seven letters to seven churches and then had each letter sent to the church where it was addressed. But go back and read 1:11 again, then read v. 19. Jesus told John to write *everything* down in a book and then send the whole book to each church! Consequently, each church got to read the whole book of Revelation, including the letters to all the other churches! Now, I don't know about you, but that lights a fire in my pants! Imagine getting a letter addressed to your church body that contains letters to other churches in your area. Imagine that the letter didn't come from some diocese or denominational headquarters. The letter came from <u>God</u>. Imagine being able to read what God says about all the other churches around, knowing that all the other churches are getting to read all the dirt on your church as well. I'm thinking that Jesus really knows how to motivate His people!

John has this personal visit from the risen King, and he wrote (here in Chapter 1) what he "has seen." Now he turns in Chapters 2 and 3 to "the things which are," the Church Age. Since our focus now is on the Tribulation, we're not going to spend any time on the Age of Grace, except to say that God's use of seven churches could be (and, to my mind, *should* be) interpreted to mean that this is representative of the entire Church Age. The number seven in the Bible indicates completeness (e.g. the seventh day, which is the day that God uses to commemorate the completion of Creation). These two chapters, which are comprised entirely of these seven letters, tell us that this is God's way of saying that this is the whole period from Pentecost up until the end of the Church Age.

I do want to make one observation here, and that is that some Bible commentators say that each church, which has its own set of strengths and weaknesses, represents a specific time period in church history. Those that hold to this position usually say that we're in the seventh and final stage of history, that being the church most strongly associated with the "lukewarm church" at Laodicea (Rev. 3:14-22). I do not hold this view. While I heartily agree that we're in the final hours before our Lord returns, I think we can identify with all of these churches throughout the whole of the past two thousand years. Suffice it to say that the Lord gave us these letters, not as a timeline, but as a report card on what He's looking for out of His New Testament body.

Speaking of which, look at the Timeline of Revelation at the end of this book. Created by my wife, this graph is located in Appendix B on page 270. As we work our way up from the bottom to the top (or from left to right, if you turn it sideways), we now come to the third item on our list, the Rapture itself. In Chapter 1, it was explained to us the things which John "had seen." Then, in Chapters 2 and 3, we saw "the things which are" (the dispensation of God's grace by way of the church). This age, as we've already seen, will come to an abrupt and unheralded halt. The last letter of Revelation 3, which was to the aforementioned Laodiceans, ends in v. 22. Do you see that very last word of Chapter 3, the word "churches"? I have that word underlined in my Bible, because it's the very last time that the church is mentioned in Revelation until 22:16, where that word is used to tell us the intended audience of the book.

Many scholars agree that the body of Christ suddenly and without warning falls off the page at the end of Chapter 3 to serve as an important message to the church at large. I agree with such scholars, and I'll tell you why. Read Gen. 14:17-20; Heb. 6:19-7:6. This strange personage, Melchizedek, walks out of nowhere onto the pages of Scripture, and after a brief exchange with Abram, walks right back off. There are several verses in both testaments that give us little insights into who this man is, but he is still quite a mystery.

The point here is that Melchizedek is a very important person, and his departure is as curious as his arrival. If you stop and think about it, the church is kind of the same way. It's not like the world was expecting the birth of the church on Pentecost, and it's not as though the world is looking for us to just up and vanish one day, either. But that's exactly what's going to happen! The day is coming when one moment the church is rolling along, singing her song, then POOF! We're gone! (The same thing was seen in Enoch, which we saw earlier in Gen. 5:21-24; Heb. 11:5.)

Just as Melchizedek and Enoch both simply fall off the page, so will we. Go back to Revelation, and read 4:1-2. That, as we've discussed previously, is the Rapture. The remainder of Chapters 4 and 5 is a picture of what we're going to be doing once our Savior calls us home, which is where we'll turn in just a little bit. Before we do that, though, I want to throw one last thing out there about the Rapture. Have you ever stopped to think about where we go when God calls us home? I mean, we know that we'll go *up*; I Thess. 4:13-17 says that we'll be caught "up" to meet the Lord in the *air*. What I'm asking here is if you've ever wondered if there is a specific direction on the compass from which our Lord will come. I always used to think that Jesus would come down from heaven and hover over Jerusalem. That opinion changed when I once heard someone toss out an idea that made good sense to me.

Go back to the Old Testament for a minute, and let's run through this together. In Leviticus 1, God gives instructions to the children of Israel on how to make burnt offerings to Him. Read Lev. 1:10-11, and take note of the directional word "north." Now jump ahead to Job 37, where Job's companion Elihu is waxing eloquent about the majesty of God. Read 37:21-22, and see once again the reference to the northerly direction. Okay, now go one more book to the right, and read Psa. 48:1-2; 75:4-7. Notice that passage in Psalm 75; it says in v. 6 that exaltation does not come from the east, west, or south. Conspicuously absent is one direction.

The conclusion of this theory is that when Jesus comes and shouts to all His saints to "Come up here," He will come and draw us to Himself somewhere along the very top of the world at the North Pole. To cement this idea, read Isa. 14:12-14. Pay special attention to what the devil says in v. 13; he says that "I will also sit on the mount of the congregation on the farthest sides of the north." I believe the preacher who introduced me to this idea may be onto something here!

At any rate, that wraps up our look at the Introduction, the Church Age, and the Rapture. Next item up is a scene in heaven, which is where we will carry out our first assignment of praising and worshiping God before His magnificent throne.

Chapter 14

Worship Before the Throne

This section of Scripture, the chapters we're about to read, should thrill our hearts. These verses give us a glimpse of the first moments we're going to have in God's presence. Let's take a peek inside the Throne Room of heaven, which is where we'll be right after the Bridegroom carries us away to the Father's house. Let's pick up the action right after the Rapture (Rev. 4:1); read vs. 2-11. There's definitely a key word in this chapter. Did it jump out at you? It's the word "throne." The word is used thirteen times in this chapter, and eleven of them refer to God's throne. The other two uses of this same Greek word "thronos" are in v. 4, and they refer to thrones being occupied by a group the Bible calls "24 elders." There is considerable debate over who these 24 elders are, although it seems to be almost universally accepted that they are representatives of a much larger group of people.

Many scholars, such as J. Vernon McGee and John MacArthur, believe that these 24 elders represent the New Testament church, which is now in heaven thanks to the Rapture. Here's what MacArthur writes in his study Bible notes on Rev. 4:4: "Their joint rule with Christ, their white garments (19:7,8), and their golden crowns (2:10) all seem to indicate that these 24 represent the redeemed (vv. 9-11; 5:5-14; 7:11-17;

11:16-18; 14:3; 19:4). The question is which redeemed? Not Israel, since the nation is not yet saved, glorified, and coronated. That is still to come at this point in the events of the end. Their resurrection and glory will come at the end of the 7 year tribulation time (cf. Dan. 12:1-3). Tribulation saints aren't yet saved (7:9, 10). Only one group will be complete and glorified at that point – the church. Here elders represent the church, which sings the song of redemption (5:8-10). They are the overcomers who have their crowns and live in the place prepared for them, where they have gone with Jesus (cf. John 14:1-4)."[1]

This might be the prevailing view among students of prophecy, but I would like to offer a different approach. Go back to Ephesians 2. In vs. 11-18, Paul describes us Gentile believers as having been brought near to God by the blood of His Son, and that the "middle wall" separating Jews and Gentiles has been torn down by His sacrifice, thus making one group from the two (vs. 14-15). In brief, the emphasis of this portion of Ephesians 2 is on turning two groups of people into one.

Now read the rest of the chapter, vs. 19-22. As I ponder this section, I get the sense that this is referring to the saints from both the Old and New Testaments. The "prophets" of v. 20 might be referring particularly to NT prophets (cf. 3:5), but it could also be inclusive of the OT prophets as well. It's my belief, although I'm far from being dogmatic about it, that the twelve tribes of Israel and the twelve apostles of the NT church are what make up the 24 elders, as that would make the two groups into "one new man" (v. 15).

Without chasing this rabbit too much farther down the trail, let's see if we can unravel this mystery together. I want to see if we can pin down these 24 elders just a little bit better. As I began studying for this section of the book, I expected to hear myself say that even though the OT and NT saints are going to be praising God shoulder-to-shoulder once we're raptured, the body of Christ isn't going to be exactly like our counterparts from the other side of the cross. I was going to say that we're going to have our glorified bodies, but I would concede the point that OT believers will still be in their temporary bodies. I was going to say that because of the "Rapture Scripture" in I Thessalonians 4.

Please turn there once again, and I'll show you the popular belief that I had embraced without really questioning the generally accepted interpretation, at least until now. Read vs. 13-17 once again. Notice the phrases "those who sleep in Jesus" (v. 14) and "the dead in Christ" (v. 16). Many dispensational scholars believe that the "dead in Christ" are only NT believers who lived and died during the Church Age. To continue in their line of thinking, go back to Daniel 12, because we find something there that talks about the resurrection of the righteous dead as well. Read Dan. 12:1-2. Going back to MacArthur's study Bible notes he says this about v. 2: "Two groups will arise from death constituting the "many" meaning all, as in John 5:29. Those of faith will rise to eternal life, the rest of the unsaved to eternal torment. The souls of OT saints are already with the Lord; at that time, they will receive glorified bodies (cf. Rev. 20:4-6)."[2]

Remember now, we're trying to answer a single question: Who are the "dead in Christ" mentioned in I Thessalonians 4? The reason we want to know the answer is that we want to know when the Old Testament saints will be given their glorified bodies. Will they be glorified when we are? Or will it be after the Tribulation? Up to now, when I started doing a little digging, I agreed with these contemporary teachers who say that the dead in Christ are only those NT believers.

Let's look at another passage that these teachers use to try and strengthen their case. Read I Cor. 15:20-23. And again, let's read what MacArthur has to say about it. Here's what he writes about v. 23: "Christ was first, as the firstfruits of the resurrection harvest (vs. 20-23a). Because of His resurrection, 'those who are Christ's' will be raised and enter the eternal heavenly state in 3 stages at Christ's coming (cf. Matt. 24:36, 42, 44, 50; 25:13): (1) those who have come to saving faith from Pentecost to the Rapture will be joined by living saints at the Rapture to meet the Lord in the air and ascend to heaven (I Thess. 4:16,17); (2) those who come to faith during the Tribulation, with the OT saints as well, will be raised up to reign with Him during the Millennium (Rev. 20:4; cf. Dan. 12:2; cf. Is. 26:19,20); and (3) those who die during the millennial kingdom may well be instantly transformed at death into their eternal bodies and spirits. The only people left to be raised will be the ungodly and that will occur at the end of the Millennium at the Great White Throne Judgment of God..., which will be followed by eternal hell (Rev. 21:8)."[3]

So far, so good, yes? It looks like the only people who get raptured are NT saints who died some time after the cross or are still alive at the time of the Rapture. But now I'm going to toss a little wrench into the machine. Turn to the right a little ways, and read Eph. 4:7-10. Now this time, I'm going to get McGee's insights on this. Specifically, here's what he says about v. 8: "'When He ascended up on high' refers to the ascension of Christ. At that time, He led captivity captive, which refers, I believe, to the redeemed of the OT who went to paradise when they died. Christ took these believers with Him out of paradise into the very presence of God when He ascended. Today when a believer dies, we are not told that he goes to paradise, but rather he is absent from the body and present with the Lord (see II Cor. 5:8; Ph. 1:23)."[4]

McGee then draws a similar conclusion about vs. 9-10: "The logical explanation of these verses is that since Christ ascended, He must have necessarily descended at some previous period. Some see only the Incarnation in this. The early church fathers saw in it the work of Christ in bringing the Old Testament saints out of paradise up to the throne of God. We are told that He descended into hell. It is not necessary, however, to assume that He entered into some form of suffering after His death. His incarnation and death were His humiliation and descent, and they were adequate to bring the redeemed of the Old Testament into the presence of God."[5]

Let me sum up the theory here. I Thessalonians 4 says the "dead in Christ" will be raised incorruptible at the Rapture, with their spirits being reunited with now glorified and perfected bodies. Since Daniel 12 and

Revelation 20 speak of Old Testament saints getting their glorified bodies at the Second Coming (along with the martyred Tribulation Saints), only the New Testament believers will receive their perfect bodies at the Rapture (which is confirmed by the passage in I Corinthians 15). So, while the OT believers are now in heaven alongside NT Christians (Ephesians 4), only NT believers will get to enjoy their perfected bodies in heaven for the first seven years we're there. Hence, you and I will be standing around the throne, praising and worshiping God, sporting our shiny new bodies, while the OT saints will be clothed in some kind of temporary bodies until the Second Coming.

The sequence of events goes like this. At the Rapture, Jesus will bring with Him the "dead in Christ," the deceased NT believers. These people – the ones who "sleep in Jesus" – will have their spirits reunited with their bodies a literal split second before the saints who are yet living on the earth. Immediately following the reunion of the dead saints' spirits with their bodies (which will be raised imperishable), the saints yet living on the earth will get their perfected bodies as well. We will all meet the Lord in the air and then return with Him to the Father's house, which is where the OT believers will have been all along, still clothed in their temporary bodies.

However, I want to jump in here and offer you a different take on that theory. To repeat, we're still trying to answer who the "dead in Christ" are in I Thessalonians 4. It seems to me that none of these scriptures say that the OT saints will be left out of the "glorified body bonanza" at the Rapture. Read John 10:15-16; Rom. 10:12; Gal. 3:28; Eph. 2:14-18. If in fact there is no difference between Jew and Gentile, if we're all one in Christ, if the middle wall has been torn down between us, then does it not make perfect sense that the OT saints whose temporary bodies were carried to heaven just before the Resurrection (Eph. 4:7-10) would also come down at the Rapture and get glorified bodies as well?

You see, my big hang-up here is with these 24 elders. I'm having a hard time agreeing that these <u>24</u> represent just the church. In my daily reading, on November 24, 2013, I was finishing up reading the Bible cover-to-cover for the tenth time in eleven years, and I came across something really big. Turn to Revelation 21, and there you'll see something special about the "Bride of Christ." Read vs. 1-2, 9-14. Now check this out. Verse 2 compares the New Jerusalem to a beautiful bride. In v. 9, an angel says that he's going to show John the bride of the Lamb. Then, starting in v. 10, John describes that bride as the New Jerusalem. Clearly it's not the structure of the city itself that is our Lord's bride; it has to be the city's collective inhabitants that make up His betrothed. In v. 12, we're told that the twelve city gates have the names of the twelve tribes of Israel written on them. I take this to mean that the OT saints are represented here. Finally, v. 14 says that the city walls have written on them the names of the twelve apostles.

I believe this speaks of the church. I don't think it's any kind of a stretch to interpret the New Jerusalem, also known as the bride of the Lamb, to be comprised of both OT and NT saints, and they're each represented by the number "12". To me, this may be the strongest case of all to say that the 24 elders are made up of believers on both sides of the cross.

If I'm right, both the Old Testament <u>and</u> the New Testament saints (represented by the 24 elders) will ALL have glorified bodies, and we'll worship around the throne with brethren going all the way back to Adam and Eve in our permanent, immortal bodies. Regardless of whether we're all wearing our gleaming new outer coverings, or if the OT folks have to wait to get theirs, we'll still be up there, praising our God and His Christ, and that with a little back-up help from God's mighty angels!

All right, let's go back to Revelation and move on to Chapter 5. Read vs. 1-7. This is a very important section of Scripture, because it helps us understand what Revelation is all about. Remember how we saw, back in Chapter 4, all those uses of the word "throne"? The word "throne" or "thrones" is used 38 times in the book of Revelation. Remember, too, that the theme of this book is the unveiling, or full disclosure, of our coming Lord Jesus. This portion, here in Chapter 5, describes what must take place before the King takes His seat on the throne of His father David in Jerusalem.

What do you suppose that scroll is, the one that caused John to weep over in v. 4? Scrolls were used for a variety of things in John's time. They were the instrument for contracts like wills, title deeds, and marriage agreements. The outside of the scroll summarized the contents of what was inside, and on the inside were the details of the document. Jer. 32:6-15 describes a deed to the land of Israel. This scroll seems to be something along those lines; I interpret it as being the title deed to the whole earth. The reason I believe this is because the 21 primary judgments of the Tribulation are all wrapped up in this scroll. It is clear that these judgments *must* take place in order for Jesus to take possession of His kingdom.

Jesus will take the scroll from the Father's hand. When that happens, that will set off another chain of events. Read Rev. 5:8-14. It seems that John cried back in v. 4 because he somehow knew that the earth wouldn't be turned over to God the Son until He had taken possession of the scroll. When He takes the scroll, we will fall down in worship of Him, for He alone is worthy! By the way, since we're now in heaven and that scroll (which contains the judgments of the Tribulation) isn't handed over to Jesus until we arrive there, that can only mean that we're taken to heaven in the Rapture <u>before</u> the Tribulation begins.

So here we all are, the redeemed of all the ages, singing praises to both the Father and the Son, and we're even singing about things to come. Verse 10 says that we praise the Lord for making us kings and priests and that we shall reign on the earth. When Jesus returns to set up His kingdom, He's coming with us and we shall reign over this earth alongside our great God and Savior!

Chapter 15

The First Seal, the Man of Sin

All right, let's move on to the next item on our timeline. We've seen the body of Christ, whose abrupt and glorious end came at the Rapture, relocate to the Throne Room of heaven. Jesus has a scroll in His hand, and we're praising His holy Name. Now we come to the opening of that scroll, which is found in Rev. 6:1-2: "Now I saw when the Lamb opened one of the seals; and I heard one of the four living creatures saying with a voice like thunder, 'Come and see.' And I looked, and behold, a white horse. He who sat on it had a bow; and a crown was given to him, and he went out conquering and to conquer." This hardly seems like a judgment. Of the 21 judgments soon to come upon the earth (seven seals, seven trumpets, and seven bowls), this first one doesn't fit the bill of a typical judgment. The only thing the text says is that some guy comes along and he conquers something and takes it over.

But in many ways, this is the worst judgment of all. None of the other judgments can come to pass unless this one does first. You see, this is the Antichrist and his revealing. How do I know this? How do I know that this is Antichrist and not Christ? Because of all the judgments that follow. Read Rev. 19:11-16. We will discuss this passage later on, but let's understand for the moment that this is our Lord Jesus at His Second Coming. Jesus comes with all His saints (which, if you're a child of God, will include you!) – v. 14 – and He Himself will destroy this Antichrist and his armies. There's no possible way that the man on the white horse in Revelation 6 can be the Christ, because the Christ is the Man on the white horse here in Revelation 19.

I need to take a little time to go over some characteristics of the Antichrist. No Church Age believer will get to meet him until he has a little run-in with the Lord Jesus at the very end of the Tribulation, but gaining some understanding of what this man will be like shall give us some insights into what to look for in these wild last days.

First, I need to define the term. The word "antichrist" or "antichrists" appears a total of only five times in the Bible, and all of them appear in I and II John. Please read these verses: I John 2:18, 22; 4:3; II John 7. The term "antichrist" means two things, because in the Greek the prefix "anti" has two meanings. "Anti" can mean "against," or it can mean "instead of." An "antichrist," then, is one who is "against Christ" as well as one who is "instead of Christ."

Here is a quick rundown of these verses that speak about this personage who is both against Christ and who desires to replace Christ. In I John 2:18, we see that there have been "many antichrists," but there is also coming THE Antichrist. In v. 22, the term is defined for us as being one who denies the Father and the Son. In 4:3, it is the spirit of the Antichrist that denies Jesus as having come in the flesh. That definition is repeated almost verbatim in II John 7.

The Antichrist will be someone who opposes Christ (partly by his denying of Christ) while at the same time trying his dead-level best to replace Christ. The verses we've read thus far don't say that; only the term "antichrist" means that. However, there are other places in the Bible that do speak to this notion of the Antichrist wanting to take over for Christ, and I want to familiarize you with a few of them. First, please read Dan. 8:23-25. Here are a number of features about this "fierce king": (1) He understands sinister schemes (so he loves subterfuge); (2) He has supernatural power; (3) He will be violent and destructive; (4) He will try to kill all of God's people; (5) He will be very prosperous (which means that no one will successfully oppose him); (6) "He shall cause deceit to prosper under his rule" (evil all around the world will be traded for good, and good for evil); (7) He will be filled with blasphemous pride; (8) He will blaspheme Jesus; and (9) He will be annihilated, but not by man. This list gives us a good picture of the coming final dictator of the world.

Go to the New Testament now, and read II Thess. 2:3-12. This "man of sin," this "son of perdition," this "lawless one," will be revealed after the removal of the Restrainer (the Holy Spirit) when the Church is called home at the Rapture. These verses give us another list we can make about the Antichrist: (1) He opposes God and exalts himself above God; (2) He will set himself up to be worshiped in the temple; (3) He will deceive the unbelieving world; (4) Through the power of Satan, he will be able to perform miracles; (5) He will be used by God to deceive those who reject God; and (6) He will be destroyed by the Lord.

Please turn to one more place. Go to Revelation 13, and let's find out about the "beast of the sea." Read vs. 1-8. How about that? Another list! We'll do this one last exercise and then compare notes with what we gathered from Daniel 8 and II Thessalonians 2. Here's our third and final list: (1) He has great authority (ten crowns); (2) He is a blasphemer; (3) His power comes from Satan; (4) He appears to have died but was "resurrected," fooling the world; (5) He enjoys killing God's people; and (6) He will NOT be worshiped by the Tribulation Saints (v. 8).

This last one touches on a very important doctrine. You and I are never to bow to anyone but God. Read Matt. 4:10; Rev. 19:10; 22:8-9. Think back to the account of Daniel and why he was thrown to lions. It happened because he refused to stop worshiping God. Shadrach, Meshach, and Abed-nego were tossed into an oven because they wouldn't worship the king. Along these same lines, Antichrist will demand worship from the world, and the world will gladly oblige. As I write this, I can think of one or two well-known people who seem to crave having the world fall at their feet. But under no circumstances will we ever participate in such blasphemy!

Well, that tells us a good little bit about this coming Antichrist. Now comes a tricky little thing, the "ten kingdoms." We'll take up this subject in the next chapter. Just turn the page, and we will begin.

Chapter 16

Ten Kingdoms and Two Witnesses

I call the notion of ten kingdoms "tricky" because a certain part of prophetic Scripture sees only one section of the world being divided into ten kingdoms, while another prophecy seems to say that the whole world is split into ten parts. Go to Daniel 7. The first part of this chapter is a vision God gave to the prophet. Daniel was shown four beasts, which represent the same four kingdoms of Chapter 2 in Nebuchadnezzar's dream about the statue (Babylon, Medo-Persia, Greece, and Rome). In 7:1-6, the first three kingdoms are described as a lion, a bear, and a leopard. Now read vs. 7-8. This is an indescribable but "terrible beast" (which is the Roman Empire).

Next, skip ahead a few verses and read about the interpretation of this fourth beast. Read 7:19-25. Verse 25 tells us about the career of the coming Antichrist, but notice vs. 23-24. Here is a description of the revived Rome, and v. 24 says that ten kings will arise from this one kingdom. If you back up and read v. 7, and then add in the language of vs. 23-24, the Scripture seems to be saying that this kingdom – this revived Rome – will be divided into ten parts. Now read Rev. 17:9-17. This is Rome we see in vs. 9-10, and vs. 12-13 indicate that these ten rulers will help Antichrist rule the whole world.

If you put all this information together, the question now must be asked: Will it just be Rome that gets separated into ten kingdoms, or will the entire world be divided thusly? Let me answer by giving you what I have gleaned from these scriptures. The Bible is clear that this revived Roman Empire will have ten kings, and these kings will assist Antichrist in ruling the globe.

But there's another passage in Daniel that gives us great insight as to the possibility that ten kingdoms, or ten provinces, will exist within the European continent. Read Dan. 2:36-43. This is the dream Nebuchadnezzar has about the monstrous, metallic statue, and Daniel is telling the king the dream and its interpretation. Verse 41 says plainly that this fourth kingdom (Rome) will most definitely be divided into ten parts. Since there will be ten kingdoms within Rome, and since there will be a king selected out of each kingdom, it would seem reasonable to deduce that the world may also be split up into ten parts in order that each king might rule over a tenth of the world. If that's how it will be, then the kings may operate independently to preside over their province but would collectively answer to the Antichrist.

At any rate, the world is now under the rule of Antichrist and the "League of Ten." Now comes two of the most colorful characters you'll ever meet, the witnesses of Revelation 11. Turn there, and read verses 1-14. The witnesses are mentioned right on the heels of the temple, so it's my belief that the duties of their ministry will be discharged at or near the temple grounds. Because these two men are mentioned in the same breath as the temple, and because the temple will be destroyed at the midpoint of the

Tribulation, it logically follows that these two witnesses will have their 1,260 days in the sun during the first half of the Tribulation.

Much has been speculated about the identity of the two witnesses, although Elijah seems to be an almost absolute certainty for one of them. Two popular suggestions for the other witness are John the Baptist (McGee casts his vote for this one) because of the fact that his ministry was to prepare the way for the coming of the Lord. Another common guess is Enoch. That's because he (like Elijah) has yet to die. However, I have a few reasons for thinking that Elijah's partner will be Israel's deliverer from Egypt, Moses. These two men will be able to send plagues upon the earth, just like Moses did. They'll keep rain from falling upon the earth for 3-1/2 years, just like Elijah did. The Old Testament speaks of a return of both Moses and Elijah (cf. Deut. 18:15-18; Mal. 4:5-6; John 1:21). Moses and Elijah were together with the Lord at His transfiguration, which was a preview of the Second Coming. Elijah was carried alive into heaven, having never tasted death (II Kings 2:11). Moses, on the other hand, died, but Satan fought hard against God's angelic commander to dispose of his body (Jude 9). It appears that God still has some work for these two men to do here on earth!

Regardless of the identity of these mighty warriors, their mission is very clear: they are to announce God's judgment to those that dwell upon the earth. That's the reason for there being two witnesses this time, instead of just the one in the case of Jesus' first coming with John the Baptist (see Deut. 17:6; 19:15). Once they're killed by Antichrist after exactly 1,260 days of ministry, they'll lie unburied in the streets of Jerusalem for 3-1/2 days. At the end of that time, they'll be resurrected and carried into heaven (i.e. raptured) in the same manner that Jesus ascended in Acts 1. Then there will be a major earthquake in Jerusalem, and it will destroy one-tenth of the city and kill seven thousand people. You could say that these two witnesses are going to be real showmen, and they'll go out with a bang!

Okay, we've been introduced to a few of the Tribulation's major players, and we've opened the first seal. Now let's go on and look at some of the judgments yet to come.

Chapter 17

Hell Pays a Visit

Returning now to the subject of the seal judgments, let us read about the second seal: "When He opened the second seal, I heard the second living creature saying, 'Come and see.' Another horse, fiery red, went out. And it was granted to the one who sat on it to take peace from the earth, and that people should kill one another; and there was given to him a great sword" (Rev. 6:3-4). These two verses are probably the best evidence for proving that the rider on the white horse in vs. 1-2 is *not* Jesus. Even though Revelation is not written in perfectly chronological order (especially as it relates to certain events during the Tribulation), the 21 primary judgments (seals, trumpets, and bowls) are presented in sequence. That must be the case because it's the only way to make sense of the judgments.

As I noted earlier, none of the other judgments can take place without this first judgment, the judgment of Antichrist and his rise to power. If the first seal is Jesus, and if he's going to rule the nations with a rod of iron (Psa. 2:8-9; Rev. 2:27; 12:5; 19:15), and if He's the King of kings and Lord of lords (I Tim. 6:14-15; Rev. 17:14; 19:16), but if He allows the world to fall into chaos and tumult right on the heels of His coming, then He'd be a most imperfect ruler, wouldn't He?

Therefore, there's NO WAY that that first seal is King Jesus! He is the Almighty God, and to Him belong all honor and glory forever! This impostor is none other than Antichrist, Satan's chief emissary, because Satan can't hold anything together; all he can do is break stuff. And that's what he does, starting with this second seal, the red horse of war. It is my belief that the Battle of Gog and Magog as described in Ezekiel 38-39 is this second seal. The timing seems right, especially since Israel will be "dwelling safely" in her land (Ezek. 38:8, 11, 14). That's clearly the purpose of the seven-year treaty of Dan. 9:27 (as we saw earlier), to create the *illusion* of harmony between Israel and her enemies.

However, no sooner does Antichrist become potentate of the nations, bringing peace to mankind, and then the very next thing to happen is war and carnage will break out in every corner of the globe. After this is the opening of the third seal: "When He opened the third seal, I heard the third living creature say, 'Come and see.' So I looked, and behold, a black horse, and he who sat on it had a pair of scales in his hand. And I heard a voice in the midst of the four living creatures saying, 'A quart of wheat for a denarius, and three quarts of barley for a denarius; and do not harm the oil and the wine'" (Rev. 6:5-6).

This is the black horse of famine. War frequently brings about famine, although it's not because of a lack of food so much as it is a lack of being able to transport it to places where it's needed. I suspect that this will be an agricultural crisis unlike any the world has ever seen, because it will be a famine that could be caused by both a lack of food supply as well as a hampered ability to get the food to the places hardest hit.

The references to the wheat and barley are indicative of the amount of food that would be needed to keep a very small family alive for a single day. Also, the "denarius" was a typical day's wage in New Testament times. The idea here is that there will be no way to make a house payment or keep basic utilities going. This is a third-world, hand-to-mouth existence, and it will dominate the entire planet. The oil, which was used to prepare bread, and the wine, which was for cooking and water purification, will no longer be staples that can be taken for granted. They'll be luxuries that probably only a wealthy few will be able to afford.

Adding insult to injury, conditions just keep getting worse. Antichrist comes in on his white horse, ready to save the day, only to bring death and destruction in almost the same moment that he takes the reins of the whole planet. Yet there is no rest for a sin-weary world, as now the fourth seal is broken: "When He opened the fourth seal, I heard the voice of the fourth living creature saying, 'Come and see.' So I looked, and behold, a pale horse. And the name of him who sat on it was Death, and Hades followed with him. And power was given to them over a fourth of the earth, to kill with sword, with hunger, with death, and by the beasts of the earth" (Rev. 6:7-8).

This doesn't need much explanation, but I want to pause here for one quick observation. See there in v. 8, where it says that one-fourth of the world's population will be annihilated? As of December 27,

2013, there were approximately 7,200,615,139 living, breathing people on the earth.[1] Supposedly, there are presently about two billion professing Christians in the world, although that number is sure to be heavily inflated.[2] According to a 2012 Gallup poll, 77% of Americans identify themselves as "Christians."[3] There are 321 million people in the U.S. right now.[4] If these statistics are accurate, that means there are 247,100,000 Christians in America. I'm going to go out on a very short limb here and say that there is no possible way that there are 240 million born-again, Bible-believing Christians in the United States right now. The current number of true "American" Christians is probably closer to between ten and fifteen percent of the population, which puts us at somewhere around 30 to 50 million.

We can extrapolate from this figure and say that, being very generous here, there are 750 million bona fide believers alive right now on planet earth. If we were raptured today, the world's population would plummet from 7.2 billion down to 6.5 billion in the twinkling of an eye.

Using the v. 8 forecast that seals two through four will cause the demise of one quarter of the world's population, that means that the judgments of war, famine, and death will bring the world's population from 6.5 billion down to 4.875 billion. That's a death toll of 1.625 billion people. Think about this for a moment. We're talking about over a billion and a half people dying during the first four judgments alone, and they're the mildest of the judgments!

All right, get ready now for a slight change of scenery. This next judgment is different from the ones leading up to it because of its action and because of its location. Rev. 6:9-11 reads: "When He opened the fifth seal, I saw under the altar the souls of those who had been slain for the word of God and for the testimony which they held. And they cried with a loud voice, saying, 'How long, O Lord, holy and true, until You judge and avenge our blood on those who dwell on the earth?' Then a white robe was given to each of them; and it was said to them that they should rest a little while longer, until both the number of their fellow servants and their brethren, who would be killed as they were, was completed."

This fifth seal is different from its predecessors because the scene shifts from earth to heaven, and because this is descriptive of the *results* of an action rather than being an action itself. Here we see the Tribulation Saints, people who come to faith in Jesus after the Rapture, and many of them are martyred for their conversion. It's worth noting here that these people will not be in permanent, glorified bodies at this point. They will occupy some kind of temporary body that I'm guessing will be like what those who died before the Rapture will have had. They won't get their bodies back and be like all the raptured and glorified saints until the Second Coming (see Dan. 12:1-2).

Now for the sixth seal; read Rev. 6:12-17. This goes back to a prophecy first uttered around 800 B.C.: "And it shall come to pass afterward That I will pour out My Spirit on all flesh; Your sons and your daughters shall prophesy; Your old men shall dream dreams, Your young men shall see visions. And also on My menservants and on My maidservants I will pour out My Spirit in those days. And I will show wonders in the heavens and in the earth: Blood and fire and pillars of smoke. The sun shall be turned into darkness, And the moon into blood, Before the coming of the great and awesome day of the Lord" (Joel 2:28-31). Here is another scene change for these judgments. God is clearly intervening with a type of judgment that only He can mete out.

It's important for me to mention one thing here, and that is the purpose of the luminaries God placed in the heavens. Go all the way back to the front of your Bible, and read Gen. 1:14-18. The sun, the moon, and every single star were put into space to give light on the <u>earth</u>. They are for seasons, for days, for years, and for *signs*. This is certainly a sign that God is giving on the earth, and it's coming from outer space (the "second heaven"). It's true that stars are way too big to come crashing into the earth (we'd get squished), so it's been speculated that this may be like meteor showers or something. Whatever it is, it will be like nothing ever seen before in history.

Finally, God takes a little breather from this parade of judgments which He has sent to test those who dwell upon the earth. We're going to take that break with Him, so turn the page, and begin a new chapter where God sprinkles a bit of grace on the world.

Chapter 18

The 144,000

God calls a brief timeout from all this devastation just long enough for Him to put a supernatural stamp on some very select men. Read Rev. 7:1-8. Notice that this sequence is prefaced with the words "after these things." In the midst of doom, despair, and agony, God gives the world a short break. He uses this time to put His protective stamp on the foreheads of 144,000 virgin men, men who will have a special mission to evangelize the world (which we'll read about in a moment).

Notice also that I said that these elect of God will be "virgins." Where did I get that? Well, jump ahead to Chapter 14, and let's see what else is said of these men. Read vs. 1-5. Verses 1-3 make it clear that the subject is these same meticulously numbered missionaries, and then vs. 4-5 give us a few significant facts about them. These 144,000 are: (1) virgins; (2) wholly devoted to following the Lord; (3) "firstfruits" (i.e. they're representative of a larger group to follow – cf. Rom. 11:25-27; 16:5); (4) committed to the truth and are therefore blameless.

There are those who like to think that their own little band is the 144,000. Jehovah's Witnesses believe that their first 144,000 converts make up *this* 144,000, with all others who've followed in their steps to be promised a similar if not somewhat less attractive eternity.[1] Seventh-Day Adventists teach that *they* are the 144,000.[2] Please allow me to dispel all such myths. The people of whom God speaks here cannot be anything but <u>Jews</u>, and they are exclusively <u>men</u>. The way in which the Bible lists them, singling them out tribe by tribe, seems almost redundant. God did that on purpose, I believe, in order that no one but these Jewish men could legitimately lay claim to being a part of this special group. There are exactly 12,000 men that will be selected from each tribe (God knows their lineage, and He'll have them set apart), and they will have a visible sign on their foreheads. The Bible doesn't say what their mark will look like, but I want to mention here that I do not believe that it will be any kind of computer chip, bar code, or electronic device. First, GOD is the one doing the sealing and marking. Second, every time a mark is used on a person or group of people in the Bible, it's always something visible (cf. Gen. 4:13-15; Ezek. 9:3-6.)

When we get to our examination of the False Prophet, we'll see the people who take the mark of the beast as an act of self-preservation. Again, I believe that this will be a visible tattoo or stamp, not a computerized appliance implanted under the skin. As for these 144,000 evangelists, they've been given a special calling, a special sign, and a special assignment. Read Rev. 7:9-17. The Tribulation will be a time of both unprecedented judgment as well as unprecedented salvation. The 144,000 will travel all over the globe, and they will lead a seemingly infinite number of Gentiles to the Lord. These new converts, or at least many of them, will be martyred for their newfound faith in Jesus. When that happens, they'll be immediately ushered (in their temporary bodies) into the presence of God. While these new Christians stand a good chance of being murdered shortly after they get saved, the 144,000 will remain under God's protection until He determines that their ministry on earth is over. That way, these evangelists can continue their ministry throughout the world.

Chapter 19

The Trumpet Judgments

Brief though it's been, that's all for the recess. (Please note, however, this isn't much of a break for the Tribulation saints; many of them will be put to death almost the minute they get saved!) Now it's time to turn our attention back to the judgments of God, starting with the seventh seal. Read Rev. 8:1-6. The primary actions of the seventh seal are an earthquake and the next set of judgments, the seven trumpets.

While we're here, I want to make a couple of observations about this section of Scripture. Notice in v. 1 that as this seal is being opened there will be silence in heaven for the space of about half an hour. Just that little phrase by itself gives us clues to several important things about heaven. First, we can see that time is very important to God. Have you ever heard anyone say that time is meaningless to God? That is a false statement. I'll give you a quick example, one of many I could use. Consider Acts 1:4-6: "And being assembled together with them, He commanded them not to depart from Jerusalem, but to wait for the Promise of the Father, 'which,' He said, 'you have heard from Me; for John truly baptized with water, but you shall be baptized with the Holy Spirit not many days from now.' Therefore, when they had come together, they asked Him, saying, 'Lord, will You at this time restore the kingdom to Israel?'"

Here we see Jesus, forty days after the Resurrection, and He's getting ready to ascend into heaven. In v. 6, the disciples ask Him if He's ready to restore the kingdom to Israel. He answers them in v. 7: "It is not for you to know times or seasons which the Father has put in His own authority." This statement alone makes it clear that time is actually very important to God. Time has no affect on Him, but He always operates within the confines of time. Along these same lines, we're shown by this verse that we won't lose our sense of time when we get to heaven.

Second, things are getting so bad on earth that all our worship comes to a complete stop. Our mouths will not utter so much as a single sound for thirty whole minutes, that's how bad things on earth will be. That also means that we'll actually be able to see what's happening down here. How much we will see and for how long at a time we'll be able to do that, we're not told. But it's evident from these few simple words that we will have a front row seat to at least some of the goings-on during this seventieth week, and what we'll be shown will horrify us. That's another way we can know that we're not in the Tribulation yet. Nothing that's going on in the world at this time, as bad as a lot of it is, would come anywhere near putting a damper on the church service they're having up there right now!

All right, it's time to pick back up with the judgments, starting with a quick look at the first four trumpets. Read Rev. 8:7-13. It's hard to get a handle on just how severe these judgments are, but they start out terrible and they only worsen with each passing event. The trumpet judgments will be worse than the seals, and the bowl judgments will be worse than the trumpets. I have heard it said by more than one person that they believe we're in the Tribulation right now, and they usually say that we're somewhere in one of these trumpet judgments. One of the reasons for that is because of the third trumpet and how it compares with the Chernobyl nuclear accident in the Ukraine in 1986. What these folks often argue is that the word "Chernobyl" can be translated into English as "wormwood."

One major problem with this notion is that the judgment starts in heaven, not earth. In addition, it poisons one-third of the fresh water sources all over the entire globe (v. 10). At Chernobyl, only two people died in the explosion, and about 30 more died in the weeks that followed.[1] It's imperative that we keep our focus here. Each of these judgments will kill many thousands, if not millions, of people. There is no conceivable way that this third trumpet (or any of the other judgments, for that matter) has ever taken place.

To top it off, remember what we discussed a short while back, that none of the other judgments can occur until the very first seal is opened. The white horse of the revealing of Antichrist is the domino that falls into all the others. Without Antichrist, not a single one of the other judgments will occur.

Okay, back to the Scriptures. Read Rev. 9:1-12, the fifth trumpet. I've heard it suggested that these locusts are metaphors for military helicopters. Me, I say they're locusts, even if they're not anything like locusts that any of us have ever seen. In v. 11, they have Satan as their king, although Prov. 30:27 says that locusts have no king. These also aren't conventional locusts because of what we read in Exo. 10:14, where we're told that there would never be another plague of locusts to destroy the land like that ever again. These locusts, in keeping with that promise, will not do harm to any of the earth's plant life (v. 4).

The point here is that these locusts are demonic, not typical. Furthermore, they have only five months to complete their mission (vs. 5, 10). Five months is the life cycle of the locust, but I think the reason for this period of time has less to do with how long locusts live and more to do with judgments from the Old Testament. It says in Gen. 7:24 that five months is the length of time that the floodwaters covered the earth. It is certainly possible that God is using this time frame in the Tribulation to point back to the Flood, a reminder to the children of Israel that God is judging the world for its rebellion against Him.

These locusts don't look like regular locusts (vs. 7-10), they don't act like regular locusts, and they will torment men (vs. 5-6) so badly that they'll want to die but they'll be unable to achieve that goal. Some say that these creatures will only attack unsaved people because of what it says in v. 4, where we're told that they are commanded to harm only those individuals who don't have the seal of God on their foreheads. Many commentators think this means that all saved people in the Tribulation will be protected from this plague, idea being that the people who are converted through the ministry of the 144,000 will also receive God's visible mark. I disagree, though, as I find a couple of flaws in that theory.

First off, I can't find anything in Scripture to support the conjecture that anyone during the Tribulation (aside from the 144,000) will receive such a mark from the Lord. (There's the mark of the beast, which we'll talk about soon enough, but that is a mark that is given by men rather than God.) Second, the mark on God's servants seems to be some sort of divine protection for them. We saw back in Rev. 7:9-10 that it looks as though many (perhaps even most) of these new Christians will be martyred almost immediately after they come to faith in Jesus. It makes little sense for God to put His stamp on people, only to allow them to die a few moments later. We saw how God's mark was indeed for the purpose of protection back in Ezekiel 9, and even wicked Cain was afforded that luxury in the same manner. All this is to say that, as far as I can tell, only the 144,000 have God's protective seal, so it's my belief that only those special men will be immunized against the locusts. In any event, the locusts will most assuredly attack the enemies of God, and they'll leave His 144,000 protected ones alone.

The next event after these dreadful locusts is the sixth trumpet. Read Rev. 9:13-21. Remember that the second, third, and fourth seals combine to kill a quarter of the world's population. This judgment, according to v. 15, will wipe out another third of the remaining people who dwell on the earth. If nobody were to die between the fourth seal and the sixth trumpet, there would still be 4.875 billion people still alive in the world. That will most certainly not be the case. I'm going to really lowball this, and for the sake of conservatism and the simplicity of round numbers, I'm going to say that the last three seals and the first five trumpets will claim "only" 875 million lives. That leaves us with four billion living people. The sixth trumpet will kill one-third of that number, or 1.33 billion more. Now we're down to just over 2-1/2 billion people left alive.

This reminds me of a man I learned about in my high school debate class; he was a clergyman and philosopher named Thomas Malthus. An Englishman, he lived from 1766 until 1834. He's best known for his having taught that the primary stumbling block to creating a utopian society was overpopulation. He formulated a theory that came to be known as the "Malthusian catastrophe" or "Malthusian nightmare." Malthus' hypothesis suggests that the earth can hold only so many people, and once this invisible threshold is crossed there will be rapid depopulation due primarily to a shortage in global food supply.[2]

What Malthus had in mind was that due to limits in the amount of fertile land in which to grow crops, the day would come that there would be more mouths to feed than there would be food that could be grown. His conclusion was that when that happened, there would be worldwide famine that would lead to the deaths of millions over a very short space of time. What Malthus failed to take into account was the exponential advances in technology that would overcome these barriers to food production and distribution. (In his defense, he had no way of knowing what the next couple of hundred years would bring in the way of this technological explosion.)

But Malthus left a permanent mark on society, as he was influential in the lives of many scientists, economists, and philosophers who would come after him. His speculations helped shape the minds of ungodly thinkers like Friedrich Nietzsche, evil dictators like Hitler and Stalin, and eugenics activists like Margaret Sanger. Malthus may have been wrong about the means by which the world will suffer such cataclysmic losses of people over a short period, but he was right in the respect that one day it will happen.

Speaking of this kind of catastrophe, how does this sixth trumpet play out? Well, based on Rev. 9:16, where it says the army was 200 million strong, and v. 14, where the location is given at the Euphrates River, many people believe that this would be an army put together in the Orient, probably China. However, the judgment that involves the Euphrates and the armies of Asia is on down the line; that's the sixth bowl judgment found in Rev. 16:12-16. In fact, that's the lead-in to the final great battle, Armageddon.

No, this judgment is exactly what it says it is; it's 200 million *demons* (Rev. 9:17-19). This sounds a bunch like the judgment of the locusts. It appears that these fifth and sixth trumpets are simply back-to-back demonic attacks on the world, packing a one-two punch. The people of the earth can only wish the fifth trumpet judgment would kill them, but they'll get their wish a short time later when the sixth trumpet sounds. One would think that this would break these people of their sins and lead them to repentance. But Rev. 9:20-21 makes clear the hardness of the human heart; most of the remaining survivors are still shaking their fists at God: "But the rest of mankind, who were not killed by these plagues, did not repent of the works of their hands, that they should not worship demons, and idols of gold, silver, brass, stone, and wood, which can neither see nor hear nor walk. And they did not repent of their murders or their sorceries or their sexual immorality or their thefts."

Now we come to the seventh and final trumpet judgment. Read Rev. 11:15-19. Here we see all of heaven proclaiming the answering of the Lord's Prayer: "Your kingdom come, Your will be done on earth as it is in heaven." The coming of God's ultimate judgment upon the entire world is also announced. Finally, we are told what makes up the seventh trumpet judgment, which (v. 19) is primarily an earthquake (apparently over the whole planet, since no location is mentioned) and a huge hailstorm.

This concludes the second set of the three sevenfold judgments. The third and most terrible set of judgments, the bowl judgments, still waits to be poured out upon the earth. Just as there was an interlude between the sixth and seventh seals, there is a temporary change of course that separates the first six trumpets from the seventh. This is now the midpoint of the Tribulation, and we will see a flurry of activity that defines the transition from "The Tribulation" to "The Great Tribulation." In the next chapter, we will examine these cataclysmic events.

Chapter 20

The Halfway Point

Go back to Daniel 9. Remember that v. 26 talks about the Antichrist ("the prince to come," who will be a native of the Roman Empire). Now read v. 27. This is where we get the definitive information that the Tribulation will last exactly seven years ("one week"). Notice that Antichrist will violate his own treaty with Israel by coming in at the midpoint of the Tribulation and defiling the temple. He'll bring the sacrifices to an abrupt end by means of his "abomination of desolation" (cf. Matt. 24:15).

There is a clear line of demarcation between the two halves of the Tribulation, and the Bible describes several things that will take place during this changeover. Let's take a look at each one. First, Satan is kicked out of heaven. He has access to God's throne today, but there's coming a time when he will be permanently removed from paradise. Read Rev. 12:7-12. The first few verses are written in past tense, so this cosmic war sounds like an event from long ago. How, then, do we know that this is actually a future occurrence? Because of what verses 10 and 12 say. Verse 10 tells us that the coming kingdom of God on the earth is right around the corner (which is an applicable statement *during* the Tribulation rather than before it), and v. 12 says that Satan will be furious because he knows his time is now very limited.

Consequently, one of the chief things that will make the second half of the Tribulation so much worse than the first half is the fact that Satan will be confined to the earth, and he won't be able to tattle to God on us any more.

The second big thing to happen at this midpoint will be Antichrist's fooling the world with a staged death and resurrection. Read Rev. 13:1-4, 11-14. Antichrist is now set to take over the world by force. Remember that Satan is the great counterfeiter. He's able to perform miracles, although his miracles are designed to deceive the world, whereas Jesus and the apostles performed miracles in order to validate their ministries (John 3:2; Acts 2:22). Satan is not particularly original; he's just a mimic, a copycat. For instance, God is a trinity: Father, Son, and Spirit. The devil has his own version of being triune. There's the "Antigod" (Satan), Antichrist (beast of the sea), and "Antispirit" (the False Prophet, the beast of the earth).

We'll be looking at the False Prophet in a little bit, but for now let's not miss the fact that Satan fakes the death and "resurrection" of his number one guy, Antichrist. This event is going to persuade the world to worship him, and the False Prophet will be the pied piper leading everyone to this worship. But like I said, let's leave this passage for just a few minutes. I promise we'll come back to the False Prophet.

This midpoint of the Tribulation is pretty action-packed! Satan has been booted out of heaven, and Antichrist is now ready to be worshiped by the world because of his cheap imitation of Jesus' conquering of the grave. Now go back to Chapter 12 for the next event. The devil's banishment is described in vs. 7-12, and v. 12 says that Satan is full of fury now, because he realizes how little time he has left before his doom is sealed. If you back up to vs. 3-5, you'll see that Israel (the woman) is the object of Satan's attention as he waits to destroy the Son of God, Israel's king.

Still in Chapter 12, now read vs. 6, 13-17. Here we see Satan's wrath against Israel and how he attempts to put her out of his misery. Much has been speculated about this "flood" in vs. 15-16. Some Bible commentators suggest that it's metaphorical of an army, a military attack. Not to be contrary, but I think this flood is nothing more and nothing less than a bona fide flood, as in a flood of water. Turn back to Daniel 9 and read v. 26. The Antichrist is going to attack Jerusalem, and his campaign will be accompanied by a *flood*. This sounds like the devil could be trying to get back at God and the Jews for what happened at the Red Sea after the Exodus. Furthermore, if you go back and read Rev. 12:15-16 again, you'll see that we are told plainly that the dragon chases Israel with a flood of water. (We will explore this flood more thoroughly much later in the book.)

Also, we have confidence that this event (and those in conjunction with it) will take place at the halfway mark of the Tribulation. Verse 6 says that Israel will be supernaturally protected for 1,260 days, or 3-1/2 years. Verse 14 uses the term "time and times and half a time." That's one plus two plus one-half, which equals three and a half, or to be more precise, three and a half *years*. This is clearly the middle of the seven years, the halfway mark of the Tribulation.

From here we just keep building. Satan's been walloped and removed from heaven, Antichrist is "killed" and brought back, and Satan goes after Israel, chasing her out of Jerusalem to an undisclosed location in the wilderness. Now we're going to go back and look at the False Prophet, who is Antichrist's trusty sidekick. Find Revelation 13 once more and read vs. 11-18. Here we see most of what the Bible says about the False Prophet and his ministry. Because so little is mentioned of him, the False Prophet is one the most enigmatic personalities of the Tribulation.

Let's take what information we have on this man and see if we can add to what we know. Remember that the first ten verses of Chapter 13 are about the Antichrist, the "beast out of the sea." Now, with v. 11, our attention is directed toward the "beast coming up out of the earth." If this were the only place in Revelation that spoke of this personage, we'd have a tough go trying to positively identify him. Take heart, because I have good news! This book actually does the heavy lifting here for us.

Follow along with me. Jesus, the Christ of God, is a *political* leader; He is the King of kings and Lord of lords, and He will rule the nations with a rod of iron. The Antichrist will likewise be a political leader who will rule the world, and he will demand that he be worshiped. Now let's make a quick comparison of the Holy Spirit and the False Prophet. For a brief refresher on the role of the Holy Spirit, flip back to John's gospel and read a couple of verses. Much of Chapters 14 and 16 discuss the coming Holy Spirit, but I want to read just a small portion of what Jesus tells His disciples in that section of Scripture: "'I still have many things to say to you, but you cannot bear them now. However, when He, the Spirit of truth, has come, He will guide you into all truth; for He will not speak on His own authority, but whatever He hears he will speak; and He will tell you things to come. He will glorify Me, for He will take of what is Mine and declare it to you'" (John 16:12-14).

The Holy Spirit's main function is to indwell the believer (cf. John 14:16-17) and thereby empower him to serve the Father and the Son. In short, the role of the third member of the Trinity is to glorify the Son through declaring God's truth to the world through His Word and through all believers. Now, with the understanding that the Spirit's job is to point us to Jesus, go back to Revelation 13 and read again vs. 12-15. Notice in v. 12 that the False Prophet forces the world to worship Antichrist. Verses 13-14 talk about his ability to deceive the world through miracles that will cause people to listen to his lies. Then, in v. 15, anyone who fails to violate the first two commandments (by worshiping Antichrist instead of Christ and by idolatry through the worship of an image) will be put to death.

You may ask, "How do we know that this "beast of the earth" is the False Prophet and the "beast of the sea" is Antichrist? Staying here in Revelation, I shall answer that question. Read 16:13; 19:20; 20:10. Rev. 16:13 identifies the unholy trinity as the dragon (Satan), the beast (Antichrist), and the False Prophet. Now take a good look at 19:20. It says there that the False Prophet "...worked signs in his (Antichrist's) presence, by which he deceived those who received the mark of the beast and those who worshiped his image." Going back to Chapter 13, we see in v. 12 that the "beast of the earth" demands that the world worship the "first beast," the Antichrist. In addition, vs. 13-14 sound very similar to 19:20 in that this second beast performs "great signs" in the presence of the world and of the first beast. Then, v. 15 makes reference to the worshiping of the image of Antichrist, which we also see in 19:20. Finally, 13:16-17 talks about the False Prophet requiring the world to take the mark of the beast, which is likewise mentioned in 19:20. It is clear, then, that this beast of the earth in Chapter 13 is the False Prophet.

This is the principal function of the False Prophet. Just as it is the Holy Spirit's job to point people to God the Son, it is the False Prophet's responsibility to lead people to the Antichrist. Up until this midpoint of the Tribulation, there are other religions that Antichrist has permitted to be practiced (although Christianity is most certainly not one of them!). That is all about to come to an end. Turn to Revelation 17 and read for yourself what is going to happen to the other false religions of the world when this time comes. Go ahead and put this book down, then pick up your Bible and read all of Revelation 17. It's all right; I'll be here when you get back.

Did you finish it? Good! Revelation 17 (along with Chapter 18), which deals with the "religious Babylon" (the harlot church) and the "Commercial Babylon" (the seat of Antichrist's government late in the Tribulation) is a source of considerable disagreement between prophecy students of every stripe. Since our objective is to stay somewhat in the arena of general highlights of the Tribulation, I don't want to get bogged down in the minutia of either of these two chapters. Keeping this in mind, we're going to scan what you just read and get the overall gist of what it's telling us.

What I'd like to do here is summarize Chapter 17 by taking it on a few verses at a time. In vs. 1-2, an angel with one of the coming seven bowl judgments speaks about the destruction of a false religious system (represented by a harlot) that has been predominant throughout the world. Verses 3-6 give a cryptic description of this promiscuous, immoral woman who flourishes on the murder and persecution of God's people.

The verses that follow give an interpretation of the first six verses. Verses 7-8 are the voice of God's messenger, who tells us that the beast (Antichrist) is at first in cahoots with the bogus religion. Verses 9-14 further explain that this "Mystery Babylon" and Antichrist's government work together to persecute the Tribulation saints. Finally, vs. 15-18 conclude the matter by saying that this worldwide religion (vs. 15, 18) will be betrayed by Antichrist, who will destroy it (vs. 16-17).

If we pull all this information together, here's how I'd condense Chapter 17 into a few brief sentences. The "harlot" is a false religion that desires to destroy Christianity. She works in concert with Antichrist from early on in the Tribulation up until the midpoint of the seven years. Then, Antichrist will turn on the harlot and wipe her out in order that he might set himself up as God.

For one last review of the major events of the halfway mark of the Tribulation, we saw these things: (1) Satan is cast out of heaven and confined to earth; (2) Antichrist acts out a ruse of his "death and resurrection" in order that he might fool the world and thereby more easily motivate humanity to worship him as though he were God; (3) Antichrist attacks Israel and causes the people of Jerusalem to flee into the wilderness, where they'll hide out for most of the remainder of the Tribulation; (4) The False Prophet forces the world to worship Antichrist under the threat of death for noncompliance; and (5) Antichrist destroys the dominant competing religion and demands that he be hailed and crowned as God.

Interestingly, there's another passage in the New Testament that says almost those exact words; just read II Thess. 2:1-12. Well, that's it for the halftime show. Now we return to the big game. We'll pick up in the next chapter with the most terrible judgments of all, the seven bowls.

Chapter 21

The Seven Bowls

This is the third and final installment of the series of seven plagues. We'll start by going quickly through the first five bowl judgments. Read Rev. 16:1-11. Here we see these intense plagues coming upon "those who dwell on the earth" in rapid succession. The first bowl causes sores like those found on Job. Next, the sea is turned into blood, followed by the same with all the fresh water. In the fourth and fifth bowls, the people of the world cry out in pain from both light (the sun) and darkness. Please notice also, in vs. 9 and 11, that the world no longer has any atheists. These rebellious, lost, unregenerate people may still be shaking their fists at God with their wicked deeds and their blasphemies, but one thing they're not doing is denying the existence of God.

This fact – the fact that these people are no longer denying God – means that God is right in saying what He does in Rom. 1:20, that men have no legitimate excuse to reject the reality of His existence. Now let's look at the sixth bowl judgment. Read Rev. 16:12-16. This is the judgment that paves the way for the last great conflict before the Second Coming, the infamous Battle of Armageddon. Verse 12 says that God will dry up the Euphrates River so the armies from the Orient may come to the Middle East.

The Euphrates, referred to simply as the "great river" several times throughout Scripture, stretches for nearly 2,000 miles across Syria, Turkey, and Iraq and helps to form the eastern boundary of the land that God will one day give to the nation of Israel. God is going to miraculously dry up the river in order that the "kings from the east" might cross over and come to the valley of Megiddo. Hence, this next to last judgment lays the groundwork for the impending clash. Please notice, however, who God uses to bring these armies to this final battleground. According to vs. 13-14, it is the unholy trinity, depicted as frogs, which will do the beckoning.

We'll talk more about Armageddon in a bit, but first I want to dispose of this seventh and final bowl judgment. Read Rev. 16:17-21. Here we have a worldwide earthquake, a temblor so powerful that it flattens the mountains and destroys the islands all over the globe. God will also be hurling hailstones to the earth, each weighing a "talent" (which amounts to about 100 pounds). To put a little perspective on this, I did some research to find out the current world record for a hailstone. As of the time of this writing (2014), a hailstone measuring eighteen inches in diameter was recovered after a nasty storm in Vivian, SD in July, 2010. It weighed in at a whopping 1.93 pounds![1] That, dear reader, is the heaviest hailstone ever recorded – two pounds! I submit to you that a 100-pound hailstone will be, um, BIG. And dense. And heavy.

This earthquake will also split up "the great city" (Jerusalem) into three parts. The quake will actually be an improvement for the region (as opposed to being destructive), as it will be the catalyst for making

Jerusalem the capital of the entire globe throughout the Millennium (cf. Zech. 14:1-9).

On the other hand, God will punish Babylon. That's the next event on our timeline. Religious Babylon, the harlot church, was destroyed at the midpoint of the Tribulation. Now, as we near the very end of the Tribulation, God will destroy the actual city of Babylon, the center of commerce and wealth throughout much of the Tribulation period. This book will not address the subject of commercial Babylon and its demise, but I'd like to recommend that you read and exegete Revelation 18 for yourself in your own personal study.

It's time now for the big finish to the Tribulation, the final scene of this seven-year "play." Read Rev. 14:17-20; 19:11-19. Going back to Chapter 14, there is a picture of the great battle against Israel. Basically, the whole entire world is going to show up for Armageddon, and it's going to be the bloodiest fight in all of history. The angel and his sickle are symbolic of God having led the nations of the world into judgment. Notice the term "winepress" in vs. 19, 20. This word picture carries us back to the Old Testament prophets and their portending of God's final judgment that is to come upon the earth. Read Isa. 63:1-6. What we see here is a description of our Lord Jesus and His righteous judgment upon the world at the end of this present dispensation, just prior to the Millennium.

Now jump over to Joel, and read 3:1-2, 9-17. This is a prophecy about Armageddon, described by the same kind of terminology that's used in Revelation. There are words like "sickle," "harvest," and "winepress," and references to being in the Valley of Jehoshaphat and near Jerusalem. These are violent, bloody scenes of the terrible battle of the nations that immediately precedes our Lord's return.

Go back to Revelation 14 again, and read once more v. 20. The battle of Armageddon will be in the Valley of Megiddo (known also as the Valley of Jehoshaphat), which will be just outside Jerusalem. We're also given the size of the Valley, 1600 furlongs, or 200 "Roman miles" (we'll talk more about the difference between our miles and Roman miles in an upcoming chapter). That is the length of the Valley of Megiddo and then some. The land of Israel stretches 263 miles from north to south, so the great battle will cover nearly all of the country from tip to tip.

This same verse (14:20) also describes the carnage, a river of blood that will reach "the horses' bridles." Why would the Bible talk about horses in battle at the time of the end? Seriously, why wouldn't the blood flow up to, say, the "turrets of the tanks"? Well, here's some food for thought. Think back to the sixth bowl judgment, the drying up of the Euphrates. Rev. 16:12 talks about the river being dried up so the armies from the east can cross it. Why couldn't they just fly over it? Why can't they just put their jeeps and humvees on a bridge and cross the Euphrates? Is it possible that these things won't happen because, thanks to the plunging of the world this deep into judgment, everyone has to resort to traveling on the backs of livestock?

I believe it's significant that we still haven't perfected any vehicles that don't require the use of fossil fuels. If I understand correctly what the Bible is telling us here, we're headed for a regression in travel technology, and this is my proof text I would use to make my case. I also would like to add that a river of blood 200 miles long by roughly five feet deep (up to a horse's bridle) should give us a tiny glimpse into what kind of violence and bloodshed there will be in this awful war.

All right, take a look once again at Rev. 19:11-19, which is Armageddon's scene that bleeds over (please pardon the ugly pun) into the Second Coming. What an incredible scene! I want to go back and savor this feast of the glorious appearing of our great God, one tasty morsel at a time. Read again vs. 11-13. As we discussed a while back, there are two occasions in Revelation where heaven is "opened." The first time is in 4:1-2, where we get a view of the Rapture. Heaven's doors will swing open for God's children when we ascend to meet the Lord in the air and are then taken to the Father's house. Here is the second time those doors come open, and that's to allow the King of Glory to go through the portal between heaven and earth.

This King will sit astride a white horse. He'll stick out from the crowd, as He will have eyes that look like they're on fire, and He shall be crowned with many crowns. But our description of this mighty Warrior doesn't end there. Pick up again with v. 13, and read down through v. 16. Verse 11 calls this rider "Faithful and True" (which can only be God Himself, as only God is faithful and only God is true). Verse 13 now attaches the name "The Word of God." Remember another writing of John's, where he wrote this: "In the beginning was the Word, and the Word was with God, and the Word was God. He was in the beginning with God. And the Word became flesh and dwelt among us, and we beheld His glory, the glory as of the only begotten of the Father, full of grace and truth" (John 1:1-2, 14).

What we see here is no longer the picture of the Jesus who humbly bowed to the will of a rebellious world, offering Himself on a cross, nailed to a tree, dying for sins that were not His. This is a fierce Soldier, an indignant God who is full of righteous anger. It says in v. 13 that He is wearing a robe "dipped in blood." That phrase is a reference to the prophecy of Isa. 63:2-3: "Why is Your apparel red, And Your garments like one who treads in the winepress? 'I have trodden the winepress alone, And from the peoples no one was with Me. For I have trodden them in My anger, And trampled them in My fury; Their blood is sprinkled upon My garments, And I have stained all My robes.'"

Then there's Rev. 19:15, which says that Jesus will strike the nations with a sharp sword that proceeds from His mouth. This kind of word picture is found in several other places, such as Isa. 11:4: "But with righteousness He shall judge the poor, And decide with equity for the meek of the earth; He shall strike the earth with the rod of His mouth, And with the breath of His lips He shall slay the wicked." Our text in Revelation 19 describes the Second Coming and the Millennium, and here we see this same kind of language depicting the Lord's mouth as an offensive weapon.

In fact, turn to another passage that employs this same imagery. Consider II Thess. 2:7-8: "For the mystery of lawlessness is already at work; only He who now restrains will do so until He is taken out of the way.

And then the lawless one will be revealed, whom *the Lord will consume with the breath of His mouth* and destroy with the brightness of His coming" (emphasis mine). Of course, there's also Heb. 4:12: "For the word of God is living and powerful, and sharper than any two-edged sword, piercing even to the division of soul and spirit, and of joints and marrow, and is a discerner of the thoughts and intents of the heart."

Finally, there's the clincher, Rev. 1:12-16: "Then I turned to see the voice that spoke with me. And having turned I saw seven golden lampstands, and in the midst of the seven lampstands One like the Son of Man, clothed with a garment down to the feet and girded about the chest with a golden band. His head and hair were white like wool, as white as snow, and His eyes like a flame of fire; His feet were like fine brass, as if refined in a furnace, and His voice as the sound of many waters; He had in His right hand seven stars, *out of His mouth went a sharp two-edged sword*, and His countenance was like the sun shining in its strength" (emphasis mine). Jesus spoke this universe into existence, and with this same power He can speak any part He wants back out again, which is exactly what He's getting ready to do!

Go back to Rev. 19:15, and look at the part where it says He will rule the nations with a rod of iron. This, too, is an Old Testament prophecy. In Psa. 2:7-9, God the Son says: "'I will declare the decree: The Lord has said to Me, 'You are My Son, Today I have begotten You. Ask of Me, and I will give You The nations for Your inheritance, And the ends of the earth for Your possession. You shall break them with a rod of iron; You shall dash them to pieces like a potter's vessel.'"

These are pictures of how it will be when our Lord returns to this world. And Rev. 19:16 is the icing on the cake, where yet another name is given to our great God and Savior: "KING OF KINGS AND LORD OF LORDS." Remember how we've been discussing that Jesus is a *political* leader rather than a religious leader? Here's what's meant by this. This entire passage is all about King Jesus, coming back to judge and make war against the puny rebellious armies of the world, who stand not a chance against Him when He comes and merely speaks them into oblivion.

There's one really nifty part that I left out, so let's go back and read it together again. Read Rev. 19:11, 14. When this passage comes to pass, you and I will have been in paradise for the past seven-plus years, worshiping and praising God and the Lamb. Now, heaven is opening for the second time, and all God's saints (who've been transformed at the Rapture) will be wearing the strangest military uniforms ever made, clean white linen. We'll be atop white horses (just like our King), and we will follow Him out of heaven on these magnificent steeds. We will fly through heaven's gates, enter the outer reaches of the universe, soar through galaxies and past stars and supernovas and black holes and quasars and asteroids. We'll scream into earth's atmosphere at blinding speed, and we'll touch down just outside Jerusalem, where we'll have a ringside seat for the climax to the battle of the ages.

Part Four

The Second Coming and the Millennium

Chapter 22

Armageddon

We hear the word "Armageddon" regularly, and we use it in conversation every now and then, but the Bible mentions it only once. In Rev. 16:16, we read: "And they gathered them together to the place called in Hebrew, Armageddon." It's the next thing in God's planner. Read now Rev. 19:17-19. This is quite graphic, isn't it? As we go speeding through the Milky Way, as we tear past Pluto, Neptune, Saturn, Uranus and Jupiter, we will see an angel. He will be "standing in the sun," and he will announce to the carrion-eating fowls of earth's atmosphere that it is now dinnertime. The birds of the air will gather together, circling overhead just a hundred feet or so above the battlefield, and they'll wait. Men will slaughter one another until the blood flows as high as the horses' bridles (Rev. 14:20). Once the massacre begins, birds by the millions will swoop down and begin to dine on both man and beast. As we saw earlier, the primary mode of transportation will be on horseback, so the most notable of the "beasts" will be equine. Men from every background and from every station will come, the small and the great, slave and free, serfs and kings.

Rev. 19:19 gives the ultimate reason for this battle: "Now the great city was divided into three parts, and the cities of the nations fell. And great Babylon was remembered before God, to give her the cup of the wine of the fierceness of His wrath." Antichrist, his armies, and even the armies who oppose Antichrist, will meet there to make war against the Lord. Jesus has always been the most controversial figure in all of history, and that won't change until He comes to take possession of His earthly kingdom. <u>Jesus</u> is the reason for this awful battle. Go back and read again Rev. 17:12-17. What a sad state of affairs man lives in. The world hates God, and they'll fight to the death to try and defeat Him.

Now we turn to the way that Armageddon ends. It ends with King Jesus destroying His enemies while we watch from the front row. Read Zech. 14:1-4; Rev. 19:20-21. Please take careful note of the fact that Antichrist and the False Prophet are thrown alive into the lake of fire, which is the permanent and everlasting place of torment. For them, there is no trial, no plea bargain, no witnesses to be called, no legal wrangling. It reminds me of what we see in John 16:8-11, where Jesus tells the disciples about the coming of the Holy Spirit: "And when He has come, He will convict the world of sin, and of righteousness, and of judgment: of sin, because they do not believe in Me; of righteousness, because I go to My Father and you see Me no more; of judgment, because the ruler of this world is judged."

The "ruler of this world" is Satan, and he has already been judged. That means that he will not have a day in court. But he has company. These two murderous men will be joined by the devil himself later on (which we'll talk about in a little while), but the same holds true for all the demons. In Matt. 25:41, Jesus talks about "everlasting fire prepared for the devil and his angels." All humans who've ever lived will face judgment, but the destiny of all the angels is already set. Neither angels nor demons will have access to God's court system.

Do you know why that is? It's because of a couple of things. First, either they sinned and fell with Lucifer before the fall of man, or they have never sinned and therefore they never will. How many angels there are, I don't know. However, I find it very interesting that Scripture sometimes speaks of "angels" and "stars" using interchangeable terms. Passages that talk about the "host of heaven" can refer to stars and other heavenly bodies (cf. Gen. 2:1; Deut. 4:19; II Kgs. 17:16; Isa. 34:4), but the term also refers to angelic beings (cf. I Kgs. 22:19; II Chr. 18:18; Dan. 8:10-11; Luke 2:13). The two verses there in Daniel actually make reference to both stars *and* angels and assigns both of them the title "host of heaven."

I would like to interject the possibility that however many stars there are might be about the same number of angels that exist. Regardless, one thing we can know for sure is that two-thirds of them belong to God, while the remaining third are already doomed to the lake of fire (cf. Rev. 12:4a). In short, they've either rebelled against God and nothing can alter that, or they haven't rebelled against Him and they never will. Second, angels are not created in the image of God (only man has that distinction). This means that sinning angels have no attorney and they are therefore without a Savior. Jesus died for sinful man; He did not die for wicked angels.

The lake of fire, which we'll look at again when we get to the Great White Throne judgment at the end of Revelation 20, will be populated by all the unsaved people of all the ages of time, all the angels who rebelled, and Satan himself. However, the first two inhabitants of the place of eternal destruction are the Antichrist and the False Prophet.

All right, let's move on. Chapter 19 closes with the statement that everyone, *everyone* in the battle of Armageddon, will be killed by the mighty sword wielded by our invincible Warrior King: "And I saw the beast, the kings of the earth, and their armies, gathered together to make war against Him who sat on the horse and against His army. Then the beast was captured, and with him the false prophet who worked signs in his presence, by which he deceived those who received the mark of the beast and those who worshiped his image. These two were cast alive into the lake of fire burning with brimstone. And the rest were killed with the sword which proceeded from the mouth of Him who sat on the horse. And all the birds were filled with their flesh" (Rev. 19:19-21, emphasis mine).

This is the tail end of the battle, which won't be much of a fight once the Lord enters the fracas. There's only one more little bit of business to tend to here, and we see that in the next few verses. Rev. 20:1-3: "Then I saw an angel coming down from heaven, having the key to the bottomless pit and a great chain in his hand. He laid hold of the dragon, that serpent of old, who is the Devil and Satan, and bound him for a thousand years; and he cast him into the bottomless pit, and shut him up, and set a seal on him, so that he should deceive the nations no more till the thousand years were finished. But after these things he must be released for a little while." The battle we face today is fought on an invisible battlefield by warriors we cannot see. There's coming a day, though, when faith shall be sight. John *saw* an angel that followed the train of saints from heaven to earth. He also *saw* a key and a chain that the angel was holding, which the angel used to tie up Satan, who John also *saw*. Then he *saw* the angel put the smack-down on the devil and throw him into a bottomless pit.

I want to pause here just long enough to say that we often hear people talk about "binding Satan." Sometimes I hear people say that they're "binding Satan in the Name of Jesus," or they'll pray to God that He "bind Satan" in some way or keep him "bound" from some person or thing or place. Friend, Satan is not "bound" today. He's on a leash, just as he's always been, but that leash God has him on is getting longer, not shorter. I often say that Satan (to continue our "canine analogy"), for much of my young life, was confined to the front porch. Time passed, and Satan was able to venture further out, an inch or two at a time, until he was able to get into the middle of the front yard. As I write this, he can make it clear across the street. During the Tribulation, the devil will be free to roam all over town. His boundaries will be far bigger than they've ever been. It won't be until the darkest hour in world history comes, at the end of the Tribulation, that Jesus will take care of the Antichrist and the False Prophet. Immediately afterward, a mighty angel will *truly* "bind" Satan.

Verse 3 says that Satan will be bottled up in this bottomless pit for a thousand years. At the end of that time, he will be released once more, but only for a little while. So, while we're on the subject of this thousand-year period, also known as the Millennium, let's start a new chapter and see what we can learn about it.

Chapter 23

The Case for a Future Millennium

Let's take this from the top; read Rev. 20:1-6. This passage is the reason – as in the only reason – for disagreement between Christians who hold the premillennial, postmillennial, or amillennial positions. Remember, the postmillennialist believes that it is the church's assignment to make the world better and better until it's good enough for our King to come and rule. In other words, we're in the Millennium right now, and we just need to get out there and "win this town for Christ" throughout the world, and then He'll come and sit upon His throne forever and ever.

As we've already seen early in the book, there are a couple of big problems with this. First, fixing the world is God's job, because man is incapable of doing it. The second point is like unto the first because we see that very thing in the world today. For the past six thousand years, we've done nothing but prove over and over again that we're utterly incapable of making the world better. Things aren't improving; they're getting worse. And that trend will continue "'Till He Comes."

The amillennial view says that there is no literal thousand-year reign of Christ on the earth. We are in a figurative Millennium right now, meaning that the word "millennium" is simply a substitutionary term for the Church Age. The adherents to this view argue that the thousand-year time frame is actually an indeterminate period, since it's already been twice that long since our Lord ascended into heaven.

The biggest problem with this theory (and there are several big problems) is that amillennialists don't know what to do with the Rapture and Tribulation. There are more than a few views within the amillennial camp on whether there will be a Rapture, a seven-year Tribulation, whether or not the church will go through the Tribulation, and so on. Most amillennialists believe in some form of Rapture that will come at the end of time, and no sooner will we all go up than we'll all come back down together, led by Jesus, and we'll begin eternity. For them, there's no "real" Tribulation (not one lasting seven years, anyway), and there's no literal Millennium, since we're in the Golden Age right now.

I'm not going to take up any more time trying to explain all that's wrong with these views, but if you've been with me since the beginning of this book, many of their errors should be obvious. Let me just say that I think God is *extremely* literal when it comes to His bringing about a real Millennium that will last exactly one thousand years. This dispensation will be headed up by God the Son, who will graciously allow the children of Israel and the New Testament church to assist Him. The best way for me to make my case for this is to let God Himself do the speaking. Read your passage again (Rev. 20:1-6), only this time read down through v. 7. Now, count the number of times these verses repeat the words "thousand years." In these seven verses, you see that term used six times. You read that right; that's six times in seven verses. Is it just me, or is God trying to tell us something here?

The people who hold other millennial views usually come back with two arguments against this being a literal and precise period of time. First, they'll say that this kind of verbiage in regard to a Millennium is not found anywhere else in Scripture. I respond to that argument as follows: (1) So what? How many times does God have to say something before He has a right to expect us to believe it?; (2) I find nothing in the Bible that in any way conflicts with the premillennial understanding of this literal time frame (I actually find only *support* for it in Scripture); (3) The term "thousand years" is mentioned <u>six times in seven verses</u>; and (4) We know for a fact that since Revelation was written after A.D. 70 (meaning that it was after the destruction of Jerusalem and the scattering of the Jews all over the globe), it necessarily follows that all the events from Chapter 4 onward must be events yet future (especially since Revelation calls itself a book of prophecy). If the judgments of Revelation have already taken place, when was that? And if Satan has been "bound" at any point during this age, when has he ever been prevented from doing his dastardly deeds for any significant length of time?

The other disagreement with the premillennial position says that "one thousand years" is a figure of speech. This argument is inherently a necessity to every position outside of the one I hold. If the phrase "a thousand years" really does mean what it says, then only the premillennial doctrine can be right. All of the other opinions take the millennial epoch to mean something other than a literal thousand years. The argument here hangs on the fact that the number "one thousand" is often applied as a figurative term. Those who hold to this teaching do indeed have several verses to back up their claim. For fun, we're going to look at a few of them. Read Lev. 26:8; Deut. 1:11; 7:9; 32:30; Job 9:3; 33:23; Psa. 50:10; 84:10; 90:4.

It's obvious that the case brought by the opponents of premillennialism isn't entirely devoid of evidence, at least so far as it goes on this one point (although it does little to deconstruct our refutation of their first argument). Where they start running into trouble is when they use that verse from Psalm 90, because when they do that they tie it to II Pet. 3:8. This is where their argument loses its punch. Please turn there, and I'll show you what I mean.

Many people use this verse to back up their claim that "time is meaningless to God," and it's not hard to see why. II Pet. 3:8 says this: "But, beloved, do not forget this one thing, that with the Lord one day is as a thousand years, and a thousand years as one day." I would counter that this is one of the most grossly misinterpreted verses in all of Scripture. One big reason I say this is because of its so-called companion verse, Psa. 90:4: "For a thousand years in Your sight are like yesterday when it is past, and like a watch in the night." While it is true that God sees time from a very different perspective than man does, it is not at all true to say that time is meaningless to God. In fact, I would argue for the exact opposite.

In Acts 1, Jesus is preparing to ascend into heaven. He has been on the earth for forty days since His resurrection, and He is saying farewell to His disciples and informing them of the coming of the Holy Spirit. We'll pick up right there and read a couple of verses. Acts 1:6-7: "Therefore, when they had come together, they asked Him, saying, 'Lord, will You at this time restore the kingdom to Israel?' And He said to them, 'It is not for you to know times or seasons *which the Father has put in His own authority*'" (emphasis mine). The ESV renders the Lord's words in v. 7 this way: "It is not for you to know times or seasons that the Father has *fixed* by His own authority" (emphasis mine). You see, it is foolhardy to suggest that time is "meaningless" to God, or to say that God operates outside of time. It's true that God uses time differently than you and I do (certain attributes of God, such as His omniscience and His eternality, have a way of causing that), but it's very clear that He does use time. In fact, He uses it more intricately and more precisely than any mere man could ever comprehend. Time is not only NOT meaning*less* to God, it is actually extremely meaning*ful* to Him!

Going back now to II Pet. 3:8, let's see if we can make a little better sense of this verse than to blithely say that this is God's way of saying that time doesn't mean anything to Him. The first thing I want to do is compare it to Psa. 90:4, since those two verses are so similar. The first connection that jumps out at us is the identical length of time, "a thousand years." However, as we start to look at these two statements side by side, we find that that is about the only substantive relationship. It is vital to note here that the intended audience is not the same. Peter is speaking to the *church* (the "beloved"), while Moses (the author of the Psalm) is talking to *God*. Moses writes that a thousand years in "*Your* sight" are like yesterday or a four-hour watch in the night.

Obviously, Peter and Moses are writing to two different audiences. While Moses is saying that he cannot fathom the infinite nature of God, Peter is saying that God does indeed operate within the parameters of time and space. Notice that Peter repeats himself here: "With the Lord one day is as a thousand years, and a thousand years as one day." This kind of repetition is frequently used in the Bible as a literary device that is designed to stress a point. If God wanted us to think that time didn't mean anything to Him or that He doesn't care to invade the time-space continuum in order to do His work, He would have had Peter write something like "With the Lord one day is as a thousand years, and a thousand years are like twenty minutes", or "With the Lord one day is as five seconds, and a thousand years are like four days." But God did not say that. He said that one day is like a thousand years, and a thousand years are like one day.

That's not all. Look at how the verse is prefaced. Peter starts out with a real attention-grabber: "…Do not forget this one thing…" The significance of this phrase cannot be overstated. Let me just go over a sampling of verses from both the Old and New Testaments with you (emphasis mine throughout). "Beware that you <u>do not forget</u> the Lord your God by not keeping His commandments, His judgments, and His statutes which I command you today" (Deut. 8:11). "Remember! <u>Do not forget</u> how you provoked the Lord your God to wrath in the wilderness" (Deut. 9:7). "My life is continually in my hand, yet I <u>do not forget</u>

Your law" (Psa. 119:109). "I have gone astray like a lost sheep; seek Your servant, for I <u>do not forget</u> Your commandments" (Psa. 119:176). "Get wisdom! Get understanding! <u>Do not forget</u>, nor turn away from the words of my mouth" (Prov. 4:5). "...<u>Do not forget</u> to do good and to share, for with such sacrifices God is well pleased" (Heb. 13:16).

These are just a few of nearly twenty verses in the Bible that use those same three words. In every one of these cases, this phrase is designed to draw to the reader's attention that this is something that needs to be committed to memory and obeyed. The point here is that Peter's admonition must be treated the very same way; we are to be sure and *remember* what Peter is telling us here, because it's important!

Now we're getting into another facet of this argument, so I would like to turn your attention to the idea that this verse is one of several "internal clocks" the Bible has. God has given us some signposts in His Word that help us to know when we're getting ready to experience a change in program (several of which we saw back in Chapters 2 through 4). II Pet. 3:8 is another such passage. I'll explain further in the next chapter.

Chapter 24

Internal Clocks

Go back to the Minor Prophets, and read the words of Hosea: "Come, and let us return to the Lord; For He has torn, but He will heal us; He has stricken, but He will bind us up. After two days He will revive us; On the third day He will raise us up, That we may live in His sight" (Hos. 6:1-2). As you consider these words, keep in mind the fact that the vast majority of the Bible's prophecies are aimed at the nation of Israel; this prophecy is no different. It's easy to jump to the conclusion that this is a reference to the Crucifixion and Resurrection, but that theory doesn't fit with the context here. Verse 2 says that the children of Israel will be revived "after two days," and they will be raised up (or exalted) "on the third day". Is that what happened on Resurrection morning? Were the Jews, as a whole, given eyes to see and ears to hear when Jesus arose? Not on your life!

As of the Day of Pentecost, which was fifty days after the Resurrection, there were only 120 people packed into the Upper Room when the Holy Spirit fell. I would submit to you that Hosea's time period of "two days" is metaphorical for a specific time period, something other than two literal days.

From here, let's build on what we already know. Turn over to John's gospel, the eleventh chapter. Most Christians know about Jesus having raised Lazarus from the dead, but this story is also analogous to a couple of other things. It is a picture of what the Lord does for all believers when He puts His Spirit in us and brings us out of the grave and makes us alive in Him (cf. John 5:24; Eph. 2:1, 4-6). The similarity, though, doesn't end there. There's another picture hidden in these verses that we need to discover. Let's start with John 11:3-6: "Therefore the sisters sent to Him, saying, 'Lord, behold, he whom You love is sick.' When Jesus heard that, He said, 'This sickness is not unto death, but for the glory of God, that the Son of God may be glorified through it.' Now Jesus loved Martha and her sister and Lazarus. So, when He heard that he was sick, He stayed two more days in the place where He was."

In v. 3, Jesus is told that Lazarus is sick. Then, in v. 4, Jesus announces that Lazarus' illness won't end in death. Now I'm going to toss in a little bit of information for you to chew on. While Lazarus is symbolic of every person who comes to faith in the Lord Jesus, he is also representative of the nation of Israel. Verse 6 says that Jesus stayed where He was for *two more days* before He set out for Bethany and the home of Lazarus. After those two days elapsed, then (v. 7) Jesus gathered His disciples and departed for Bethany.

Don't forget what we saw in Hosea 6, that God would rescue the children of Israel "after two days," the same length of time that Jesus waited after hearing the news of Lazarus' severe condition. Now skip down to the part where Jesus and the twelve arrive at their destination. John 11:17: "So when Jesus came, He found that he had already been in the tomb four days."

Got the picture now? Word reaches Jesus that Lazarus is deathly ill. But instead of going to Lazarus right away, Jesus hangs out for two more days (which is sure to have driven the disciples nuts!). Then, on the third day, He gets up and travels toward Bethany. By the time He gets there, Lazarus has been dead and buried for four days.

Time now for a little pop quiz. How long has Israel been around? Abram was called of God about 2000 B.C., roughly 4,000 years ago. There have been 6,000 years of human history. The first 2,000 years were spent with man in his sinfulness. Throughout the following 2,000 years, beginning with Abram, God was present with man on the earth by way of His personal interaction with His chosen people. After that, Jesus came, died, and rose again. Since that time, the world has experienced the Age of Grace, also known as the Church Age.

After the first two thousand years of history, God intervened and rescued man through Abraham. Another two millennia passed, and God sent His perfect Son into the world. Israel rejected this Man – their Messiah – so God turned to the Gentiles and gave us two thousand years of the Church Age. Now the whole world has begun to turn on Jesus, so there will be a short period (seven years) of harsh judgment over the whole earth. After that, God the Son will return and take His throne in Jerusalem, where He will reign over the entire universe for a thousand years.

Are you still with me? We're continuing to build. The book of Hebrews makes much out of the subject of "God's rest." This is Heb. 3:7-11: "Therefore, as the

Holy Spirit says: 'Today, if you will hear His voice, Do not harden your hearts as in the rebellion, In the day of trial in the wilderness, Where your fathers tested Me, tried Me, And saw My works forty years. Therefore I was angry with that generation, And said, 'They always go astray in their heart, And they have not known My ways.' So I swore in My wrath, 'They shall not enter My rest.'" This is taken almost verbatim from Psa. 95:7-11, but there is more that the author of Hebrews writes in regard to this "rest."

Keep reading the rest of Chapter 3 and on into Chapter 4. Now look at Heb. 4:3-5, which repeats part of the quotation from Psalm 95, but then it also borrows from the creation account of Genesis (Gen. 2:2; cf. Ex. 20:11). Look at these verses with me: "For we who have believed do enter that rest, as He has said: 'So I swore in My wrath, They shall not enter My rest,' although the works were finished from the foundation of the world. For He has spoken in a certain place of the seventh day in this way: 'And God rested on the seventh day from all His works'; and again in this place: 'They shall not enter My rest.'"

Do you see the connection here? God ties the six days of creation and the seventh day of rest directly to the "rest" that He promised to His children, the nation of Israel. The word "rest" is found – get this – ten times in Heb. 3:7-4:10. On nine of those occasions, the word used is a Greek word that simply means "repose" or "rest." There's one use of the word, however, that stands out. In 4:9, the word here ("sabbatismos" in Greek) speaks pointedly to a Sabbath, or "seventh-day," rest. It is a direct reference to the Sabbath rest of God first mentioned at the close of creation (Gen. 2:1-3).

While you're thinking about that, think about this: "For if Joshua had given them rest, then He would not afterward have spoken of another day. There remains therefore a *rest* for the people of God" (Heb. 4:8-9, emphasis mine). As I read this passage in its entirety, and as I give special consideration to the unique word for "rest" in 4:9 (which is used only this once in all of the New Testament), I find it perfectly rational to conclude that this is a case for the Law of Double Fulfillment. There is the immediate accomplishment with the person who gets saved and enters into the rest of the Lord right away, but then there's the connection with the literal "seventh-day rest" (or "Sabbath") as well.

If a thousand years can be represented as a single day (II Pet. 3:8), and if there have been six thousand years of human history with a thousand more left to go (the Millennium), it makes sense to conclude that this section of Scripture is pointing us directly toward the understanding that human history is a reflection of the six days of creation followed by a single day's Sabbath rest.

Take this interpretation back with you to Hos. 6:1-2, where we saw that the Lord will rescue His people "after two days." God rescued the world through Abraham after the first two thousand years of history. Then He rescued us again after another two thousand years with the sacrifice and resurrection of His dear Son. Now, two thousand more years have passed, and He's poised to bring salvation to all who are His. The only thing that remains now is the thousand years of "Sabbath rest," which is sure to come much sooner than what most of this world's inhabitants think.

This also helps us understand the phrase in Hos. 6:2 where it says that God will raise up His children on the third day, and that they will live in His presence. God will surely exalt Israel at the beginning of the Millennium, for they shall be the chief of all nations, and their Messiah shall be King over everyone and everything!

The model is simple: six thousand years of sinful man followed by one thousand years with the Righteous Judge is the equivalent of six days of the work of creation followed by one day of rest. If "one thousand years" and "one day" are interchangeable terms, which is precisely what I think II Pet. 3:8 is telling us, then we all need to be making ourselves ready. The Bridegroom is preparing to come and collect His bride!

Chapter 25

We Shall (not) All be Changed

Before we go into what this thousand-year Sabbath looks like, it's important to remember that there will be not one, but two kinds of people that will enter into the Millennial Kingdom. There will be glorified people, and there will be mere mortals. If you're a child of God, and if you're reading this book before the Rapture, you will absolutely, positively be counted among the glorified. Paul explains: "Now this I say, brethren, that flesh and blood cannot inherit the kingdom of God; nor does corruption inherit incorruption. Behold, I tell you a mystery: We shall not all sleep, but we shall all be changed – in a moment, in the twinkling of an eye, at the last trumpet. For the trumpet will sound, and the dead will be raised incorruptible, and we shall be changed. For this corruptible must put on incorruption, and this mortal must put on immortality. So when this corruptible has put on incorruption, and this mortal has put on immortality, then shall be brought to pass the saying that is written: 'Death is swallowed up in victory'" (I Cor. 15:50-54).

Before we leave planet earth in the Rapture, our humble bodies will be changed into perfect, sinless, immortal bodies. Phil. 3:20-21 gives us the same kind of information: "For our citizenship is in heaven, from which we also eagerly wait for the Savior, the Lord

Jesus Christ, who will transform our lowly body that it may be conformed to His glorious body, according to the working by which He is able even to subdue all things to Himself." Once we enter into the presence of the Lord at the Rapture, our bodies will be perfected. We'll never get any older, we'll never get sick, we'll never get gray hair or wrinkly skin, we'll never put on weight, and we most assuredly will never die. We won't sneeze, cough, burp, yawn, hiccup, or clear our throats! As we saw earlier, all believers who died before the Rapture will have their bodies resurrected and reunited with their spirit. By contrast, all Christians who are still alive at the time of the Rapture will bypass the body/spirit reconnection, seeing as to how they'll never have had those two entities separated through physical death.

So the first type of person that will be found in the Kingdom is the person who's been glorified and perfected, sinless and without any future chance of decay or death. The other type of person who will enter the Kingdom will be the one who gets saved during the Tribulation and is spared martyrdom. There are two places in the gospels where Jesus describes an event that sounds "rapturesque" (to coin a word), but in reality they are explaining His Second Coming and a description of judgment. The first of those places is found in Matt. 24:36-44; read that section, paying close attention to vs. 40-41. At first reading, it sounds like the people "taken" are those that would be snatched up in the Rapture. Remarkably, though, that is not the case. Remember that Matthew 24 is the Olivet Discourse, and Jesus is speaking there of the Tribulation. He is not addressing the church; His audience is the Jews. Now go to Luke 17, the other place where this event is mentioned, and read vs. 26-33 in order to set the scene.

Now read vs. 34-37: "'I tell you, in that night there will be two men in one bed: the one will be taken and the other will be left. Two women will be grinding together: the one will be taken and the other left. Two men will be in the field: the one will be taken and the other left.' And they answered and said to Him, 'Where, Lord?' So He said to them, 'Wherever the body is, there the eagles will be gathered together.'" We see here the reason we know that this is not the Rapture. The entire picture being drawn here is one of judgment, as it is described by the references to Noah and Lot (vs. 26-28). Then v. 37 tells us the place where the ones "taken" will actually be sent. The disciples ask Jesus where the taken people will go, and He answered with a graphic reply: "Wherever the body is, there the eagles will be gathered together."

Think back to the end of Armageddon, where we saw in Rev. 19:17-18 that an angel rings the dinner bell for the birds, calling them to come and feast on the corpses of the people claimed in the battle. Evidently, no matter where anyone is in the world at the time of the Parousia, all people doomed to destruction will be yanked up and thrown into the Valley of Megiddo, where they will be killed and then consumed by the birds of the air.

Those who are "left" (i.e. not "taken") will be left here on earth to help set up our Lord's Kingdom. These will be all the people who will have gotten saved during the Tribulation, miraculously made it to the end of the seven years, and will see King Jesus as He leads the charge from heaven to earth. These people will enter the kingdom in earthly bodies, bodies like you and I have today. Unlike us, who will be in our glorified state, the Tribulation Saints will find themselves in the boat that all the redeemed of God currently occupy. They'll be subject to temptation, sin, sickness, and ultimately, death. If a married couple enters into the Kingdom in this condition, they'll still be married. Those who go in without a spouse will be able to marry, and all such people will be capable of procreation. Their offspring, in turn, will be able to repeat the cycle.

Keep in mind that if you are a Christian, you have a *zero percent chance* of falling into this second category of people. Whether you live or die before the Rapture, you <u>will</u> be glorified the instant the trumpet sounds! That is to say that you will leave behind all earthly encumbrances, namely your propensity for sin and the mortality of your body. Only those people who become followers of Jesus during the Tribulation and survive all the way to the end will fall into this second category. As we go through the Millennium, keep this thought in mind.

Chapter 26

The Millennium as Seen Through the Eyes of Isaiah

Let's turn our attention now to the thousand-year reign of Christ on the earth. One book of the Bible, far more than any other, illumines us as to what this Golden Age will be like. In case you haven't guessed it yet, I'm speaking of the great book of the prophet Isaiah. Nearly everything we discuss in this chapter about the Kingdom Age will be drawn from this prophetic Old Testament book.

To catch things up in our chronology, we've been raptured into heaven, there was the seven-year Tribulation and ultimately the battle of Armageddon, we've all returned to earth trailing behind our great God and Savior Jesus Christ, and He has just destroyed all His foes. Antichrist and the False Prophet have been taken alive and thrown into the eternal lake of fire, and Satan has been locked away in the bottomless pit. Now we come to the Kingdom Age, a thousand years of righteousness and unimaginable success and industry, all of which is superintended by Jesus. Here are some of the things we can expect to see and experience in this glorious economy.

First, God will restore the faithful remnant of Israel to her land, the land promised to Abraham and his descendants through Isaac and Jacob (Isa. 1:25-27; 4:3; 10:20-23; 11:10-12; 14:1-2; 26:1-4; 61:1-4). That last reference, from Chapter 61, is the completion of the Law of Double Fulfillment for the Messiah and His job description. Go back and read Luke 4:16-21. Jesus fulfilled Isa. 61:1-2a in His first coming, and He'll discharge the duties outlined in vs. 2b-4 when He comes back (cf. Heb. 9:28).

It is imperative that we never forget the importance of God's covenant people in the Millennial Kingdom (cf. Jer. 31:31-34; Rom. 11). God will defeat Israel's enemies and at the same time protect her from all harm (Isa. 4:3-6; 9:3-4; 14:1-2; 26:4-5; 33:22; 35:4; 66:16). Included in that protection is the promise that she will greatly prosper (Isa. 26:15: 35:1-10; 40:11; 46:13; 49:10; 54:2-3; 55:1; 60:5, 16, 21). We must also keep in mind that Israel is important to God right this minute. Read the passages in Jeremiah 31 and Romans 11, and you will see that there has never been a time that God has forgotten about His chosen people.

If the Jews hold a special place in God's plan for the future, then we must recognize that He has a place for them right now as well. I want to continue to drive home the point that as we draw ever nearer to the Rapture and Tribulation, the days will keep on growing darker for Israel. The world will press in around them, and they will appear to have no hope. However, they shall not be moved out of their place ever again; Israel is in her home to stay (Isa 11:11). That's one way God brings glory to Himself; He waits until a situation looks utterly hopeless, *then* He steps in and rescues His people!

This leads me to the next point, that Israel will be the principal nation of the world (Isa. 54:1-3; 55:5; 56:6-8; 60:5-9), and Jerusalem will be the capital city (Isa. 2:2-4; 40:9; 60:1-5, 13-18; 62:1-7). In turn, the Jewish nation will glorify the Lord (Isa. 52:1; 60:21). In Deut. 7:6-7, God tells His people that He chose them for Himself and that He has placed them above all other nations. He goes on to explain that He didn't choose them because they were great or mighty, but rather because they were *beneath* the people groups around them.

In other words, God glorified Himself by raising up a weak, rebellious, inconsequential group of people and making them into the greatest nation in the world! If you stop and think about it, that's exactly what He's been doing with them once again. A puny little dot on the map sits smack-dab in the middle of a host of countries that hate them and want them all dead and forgotten, yet here they stand, unmoved and unmovable. God is glorifying Himself once again in this day and hour through His special chosen people, and He will use them to bring even greater honor and glory to Himself throughout the Millennium!

Thanks to her exalted position, Israel will be a blessing to the Gentiles (11:10; 19:24-25; 42:6; 49:6; 60:1-3; 61:5-6). The passages in Chapters 42, 49, and 60 explain how Israel has always been destined to be a "light" to the Gentiles, the rest of the world. What these verses mean is that it has always been God's intention that the descendants of Jacob would lead the world to Him. Up to now, that mission remains incomplete, but the Jews will fully accomplish their task when the Kingdom comes (Isa. 2:2-4).

Just as Israel will ultimately realize all of what God has planned for her, Jesus will do likewise. His rule will bring true and lasting peace (Isa. 2:4; 9:5-7; 26:12; 32:18; 66:12-13). He shall be the head of the government, and all the redeemed of God will work actively together with Him and under His authority (Isa. 9:6-7; 11:1-5; 16:5; 16:5; 32:1; 42:1-4). Remember, too, that we are praying for God's will to one day be done on earth as it now is in heaven. With our Lord on the throne of David, righteousness throughout the world will be at its highest since the fall of man (Isa. 28:16-17; 32:15-17; 45:8; 51:4-5; 61:11).

Of all the people who get saved during the Tribulation, only a tiny minority will survive and enter into the Kingdom in their mortal bodies. They will live extraordinarily long lives, marry, and have families (Isa. 65:20-23). Furthermore, everyone (and I do mean *everyone*) will know the Lord (Isa. 11:9; 19:21; 40:5; 45:5-6, 14; 52:10; 66:23).

A fascinating element of the reverse of the curse is that man isn't the only creature who will benefit from its having been lifted. Nature will prosper like it did in Eden, and wild animals will once again be tamed (Isa. 11:6-9; 30:23-26; 35:1, 6-7; 41:18-19; 43:19-20; 55:12-13; 65:25).

Ultimately, the Millennial Kingdom will be replaced by the eternal one, the new heaven and earth (Isa. 24:23; 51:6; 60:19; 65:17). We'll talk more about the eternal state – the final dispensation – in just a few chapters. It's a fair question to ask, "Why will there be a Millennium?" There are several reasons, to be sure, but let me just give you a sampling. First, it is the fulfillment of promises that God made to the patriarchs Abraham, Isaac, and Jacob. (See Gen. 12:1-3; 15:18-21; 26:1-5; 28:10-15.) Second, it's a direct answer to the Lord's Prayer, which begins with the words: "Our Father in heaven, Hallowed be Your name. *Your kingdom come. Your will be done On earth* as it is in heaven" (Luke 11:2, emphasis mine; cf. Matt. 6:9-10).

A third reason for the Millennium is that God has promised to redeem creation. There are 1,189 chapters in the Bible. The first two chapters describe creation, the last two describe the new creation, and the 1,185 chapters in between are the story of man in his sin, his failed attempts to get himself out of that sin, and God's redemptive work through His Son that bridged that unbridgeable gap. Paul gives us a condensed version of this in Rom. 8:19-22, where he explains that the entire universe is presently crushing under the weight of the curse but that one day it will all be restored. God is going to bring about a "regeneration" or a "time of refreshing and restoration" for the whole earth, and He will do it in the Millennium (cf. Matt. 19:28; Acts 3:19-21).

Finally, God will use this thousand-year period to show once and for all time just how desperately wicked man is. God the Son will rule this entire universe from Jerusalem for ten centuries of uninterrupted peace, prosperity, and righteousness, but at the end of it all Satan will be let out of his prison and he'll be given a short time to deceive the world. There will be no more need to discuss how strong the pull of man's sin nature truly is. Remember, man's first sin occurred in a perfect place, with perfect bodies and minds, and in the very presence of God. If man can fall in an environment like that, how much easier is it for him to fall when he lives inside a fallen body with a fallen mind in a fallen world? (Don't forget that only the people yet to be glorified will be able to fall into sin. If you go in the Rapture, you'll have your glorified body <u>and</u> a perfect, sinless nature from that moment on. You'll never rebel against God again!)

When it comes to this fourth reason for the Millennium, which is the proof of the significance and power of the work that Jesus did on the cross, more needs to be explored and discussed. Therefore, I want to redirect your thinking now to the end of the Kingdom Age and the release of Satan.

Chapter 27

The Devil's Swan Song

Now that we've wrapped up our time in the Millennium, we're inching our way toward the finish line. Going back to Revelation, we now set our sights on the final release of Satan. If you project back to the Parousia, one of the tasks our Lord will have completed is the binding of the devil for a thousand years in the bottomless pit (Rev. 20:1-3). At the end of that time, Satan gets one last opportunity to deceive the unsaved of the world (Rev. 20:7-9). Once he has gathered his army, they will surround Jerusalem in a battle known as Gog and Magog. It won't be much of a fight, though, because God will destroy them all in an instant!

You may recall that this is the second mention of Gog and Magog. Think back to Chapter 17, where I postulated that a battle bearing that same title will have been fought way back in the early part of the Tribulation, when Jesus opened the second seal (the red horse of war). That initial "Gog" campaign is described in Ezekiel 38-39. This battle, however, is at the end of the Millennium, and it is the final act of defiance made by the evil one.

At the end of the previous chapter, we briefly discussed several reasons for Jesus' earthly kingdom, which is sandwiched between the current dispensation (the Church Age) and the eternal state. The fourth and final reason I gave was so God could show us the power of the cross, which is what He used to break the spell of evil that blankets the entire universe. God will release the devil in order that he might go out and deceive the world one last time before he is cast into the lake of fire. By the way, in addition to God taking this occasion to prove to all humanity just how wicked the human heart is (Jer. 17:9), this is also a time where God will put His power on display, as He will destroy both the devil and all his works without even breaking a sweat.

We also need to keep in mind the fact that, even after all seven thousand years of history, Satan won't have changed so much as one tiny little bit. He will never change because he cannot change. Satan, because he is an angel and not a man, has no one to redeem him. I remember back in the days when I was still a new Christian, how I used to sometimes pray for Satan to get saved. While that may be a nice sentiment, it's a total waste of breath to offer up such prayers. Remember, Satan was judged long ago (John 12:31; 16:11), and his defeat was made certain when the Lord was crucified and resurrected (cf. Col. 2:13-15; Heb. 2:14-15).

The devil, then, is going to be released, not because there's any hope for his salvation, but so he can try one final time to stick his finger in God's eye. Going back to our text in Revelation 20, we see that Satan will have a huge following, just as he always did throughout the rest of history. In v. 8, it says that there will be as many people rise up in rebellion as there are sands of the sea. It turns out that Satan is not the only one who hasn't changed after all this time.

The first of the Ten Commandments, found in Exo. 20:3, is eight simple words: "You shall have no other gods before Me." I want to camp out for a moment on that word "before." We see that same word used a bunch of times in the Old Testament. I want to give you a couple of them here. In Gen. 6:13, God says to Noah that "...The end of all flesh has come *before* Me..." In Gen. 10:9, that same word "before" is used twice to describe Nimrod, who was called a "mighty hunter *before* the Lord."

That word "before" literally means "in the face of." When the Bible speaks of Nimrod being a mighty hunter before the Lord, it's saying that Nimrod is actually "getting up in God's face." Have you ever gotten really indignant with someone and gotten right up in their face? You know, that nose-to-nose kind of thing. That's what Nimrod was doing. To say that Nimrod was before the Lord was not a compliment to Nimrod. It's a Hebrew idiom that is conveying the idea that Nimrod was a bold rebel who wasn't about to take any guff from anybody, least of all God.

There's also another use of the word "before," although it is not the same word in the Hebrew language. In Prov. 15:11, a different word but with a very similar meaning is found: "Hell and Destruction are before the Lord; So how much more the hearts of the sons of men." This verse says that hell itself is "before the Lord." The inhabitants of hell are those who got up in God's face and spit in His eye. Incredibly, though, that verse goes on to say that the hearts of men are even more defiant against God! Satan is being let loose here, at the end of history, to be used of God to gather those that are "Before Him" together in order that they might all be judged. In a way, it's not unlike what happened when the rains came upon the earth for forty days and forty nights.

Another reason for this last hurrah for the devil could be to show all of God's redeemed what it is He saved us from. When Adam and Eve fell (as I noted earlier), they fell in a perfect environment in perfect bodies in the presence of the Creator. They had known no sin, so they weren't already bent toward it. They literally walked and talked with God. There was nothing anywhere in creation, no world system in place, to lead them down the primrose path. All they needed was the gentlest little nudge from the serpent.

Today, you and I find ourselves warring against our sinful natures, struggling mightily with a fallen world, and tempted relentlessly by the god of this age. It's no wonder we're all in such a mess! But the Millennium is the reversal of the curse and its devastating effects. And yet, there will be a countless number of people who will have been born and raised in the Kingdom who will be just like Nimrod, just like we all were until the day the Lord called us and drew us to Himself.

The battle of Gog and Magog will show us all the purity and intensity of Satan's evil. It will show us the depth of sinful man's love for iniquity and his hatred toward God. And it will show us in unvarnished clarity what God saved us from and the importance of the lengths He went to in order to buy our pardon.

Going back to our text (Rev. 20:7-9 again), we see that this "battle" won't take long at all. Masses and multitudes have gathered to attack Jerusalem, the "beloved city" of v. 9. In one swift move, God comes down in a flame of fire and consumes every last one of them. Dead, Dead, Deadsky! Now, for the big finish, we see the decisive and climactic end of our adversary. Rev. 20:10: "The devil, who deceived them, was cast into the lake of fire and brimstone where the beast and the false prophet are. And they will be tormented day and night forever and ever." No one is in the final hell (or final heaven, for that matter) today. Everyone who has ever died is presently in either an "intermediate heaven" or an "intermediate hell." We'll be looking at the final abode of God's people, the New Heaven and New Earth, in just a bit. But the current dwelling place of those to be condemned is a temporary place called "hell."

Before you start to pick up rocks to stone me for heresy, let me tell you that just because the "present hell" is temporary, that doesn't mean that the punishment for those consigned to hell is temporary. In fact, we're going to pick up that thought starting on the very next page. Perhaps the single worst aspect to the suffering of those who die apart from God is that their torment will never, ever end. Never.

Chapter 28

The Fate of the Devil and His Minions

I'm starting a new chapter here, but we're still in the same passage of Scripture (Rev. 20:7-10). Keep your eyes on v. 10 for just a little bit longer. Notice that the Scripture says that the devil had "deceived them." (The "them" are the people of vs. 7-9 who were enticed by Satan in his final attempt to get back at God). Hold your place, and go back to the front of your Bible. Genesis 3 is all about the fall of man in Eden. The first section of that chapter tells of Adam and Eve eating the forbidden fruit, which is followed by their effort to cover their shame with some fancy new leafy togs. Now read vs. 8-13. Adam and Eve, up until this point, literally "walked with God." But now, in the shadow of their rebellion, they try their best to get away from their Creator. In response, God calls out to Adam and coaxes him out of hiding. Adam and Eve then begin to play the blame game and they start pointing fingers.

Take note of the sequence of events here. Satan tempted Eve, and then Eve persuaded Adam. In v. 12, Adam blames God for having given him the woman, and in the next verse (v. 13) Eve tells God that she ate of the fruit because "the serpent deceived me." This whole mess of sin began when Satan *deceived* the woman, and the entire universe has been fighting an uphill battle ever since. Just as the devil started it all with deception six thousand years ago, he will end his campaign against God with deception at the end of time.

Going back to Rev. 20:10, we learn of Satan's final act of defiance, which follows his release from prison. Satan has always been on a leash, but throughout the Millennium he will be locked away in the bottomless pit. As time begins to run out on the Kingdom Age, he will be put back on his chain and released just long enough to deceive the world all over again. Once he does that and the war is over, his leash will no longer be a relevant apparatus. The devil will be thrown into the permanent hell, the lake of fire, and there he shall remain for all eternity.

Don't overlook this very important statement near the end of the verse. It says that Satan will be joining Antichrist and the False Prophet in that awful burning lake, which is where those two wicked men will have already been for a thousand years. As long as that time period is, it will mean nothing to them. That's because they will continue to be tormented there "day and night forever and ever." It's been asked, many times I'm sure, why there will be a change of scenery from "hell" to a "lake of fire." I like the answer the late Adrian Rogers gave to that question; I'll give you a close paraphrase of what I once heard him say in a sermon on the radio. If you're a criminal and you get arrested for having committed a crime, you're taken to jail. Depending on the severity of your crime, you may or may not be released from jail until you are tried for the charges against you. Once the trial is over, you'll be set free if you've been exonerated. However, if your guilt is confirmed by the court, you'll be sent to prison. This is a lot like that. If you don't have the right lawyer, you'll be found guilty and sent to prison.

Rogers said that when you die, you'll either be automatically set free by the blood of the Lamb or you'll be under arrest and thrown in hell, the temporary jail, where you will await trial. In I John 2:1, we're told that Jesus Christ the righteous is our "Advocate." This means that He's our defense attorney. If you are in Christ, you will be immediately exculpated of all your crimes and be with Him for all eternity. If you're without Christ, you'll be jailed in hell until you have your day in court. There, you will be found guilty, because you are guilty, and from God's courtroom you'll be transferred to prison, the eternal lake of fire.

I think that's an outstanding explanation from Pastor Rogers. You'll notice that none of the evil trinity actually gets to appear before the Judge. That's because of what it says in John 16:11, which explains that the devil has been judged already. All three of them will bypass due process and be sent straight to the lake of fire (with Satan trailing Antichrist and the False Prophet by precisely a thousand years).

I want to add one more thing here. Have you ever heard the term "annihilationism"? I had a professor in a couple of classes I took in college who subscribed to the annihilationist belief. It's a big word, but all it means is that God, after a little while of watching people suffer in the lake of fire, will have pity on them all and destroy them completely in order to put an end to their misery. The idea here is that God, in His compassion, will feel sorry for those in torment and He'll fix it so it was as though they'd never been born. Billions of human lives will be extinguished, not unlike that "blowing out the candle" concept believed on by Buddhists and Hindus.

I see at least four problems with this doctrine. First, I have never found anything in the Bible that even remotely supports that. Second, this belief makes a mockery of the cross. To whatever degree the unsaved man is spared eternal punishment, that's the same degree to which the crucifixion of our Lord was unnecessary. If the worst we would ever face in eternity is a finite time period of punishment, no matter how long (so long as it's finite), then why would Jesus have gone to all that trouble? Our sin puts an eternal distance between us and God, and only an eternal God providing an eternal sacrifice can bridge such a gap between Himself and His people.

Here are two more really big reasons why annihilationism is a heretical doctrine. I find them both in our current verse, Rev. 20:10. The third reason is that this verse plainly says that the devil is a thousand years behind the beast and the False Prophet in his entrance into the lake of fire. Antichrist and his sidekick have been broiling on the high setting throughout the entire duration of the Millennial Reign when Satan comes in for a swim, and the verse says that there's no end to their punishment anywhere in sight. In fact, that leads me to the fourth reason, where the verse ends with the statement that "...they will be tormented day and night forever and ever." The words "forever" and "ever" are actually the same Greek word, "aion". It's where we get our word "eon". It would actually be best to translate this last portion of Rev. 20:10 with the words "forever and forever."

To crystallize this idea even more, jump ahead a little bit and read Rev. 22:1-5. See where this passage ends with those exact same words, forever and ever? It's that word "aion" again, and it's used in the exact same manner as it is to describe the eternality of the punishment in the lake of fire. If the torment of the wicked is cut short of eternity by any length of time, then the same must be said of our reign in the New Heaven and Earth. We, too, will have to be annihilated. However long "forever and forever" means for the judgment of the lost, it is the same length of time for the felicity of all who have been saved. That makes no sense logically, nor is it supportable by the Word of God.

All this is to say that the destruction of the unholy trinity will never, ever end. But what about all the lost humans of all the ages; what will their fate be?

Chapter 29

The Second Death

Satan's last stand does not end well for him. The same holds true for the beast out of the sea and the beast out of the earth. Now we shall see what the judgment of all of unsaved mankind looks like. Going back to Revelation 20, we'll pick up where we left off. The next section, vs. 11-15, describes one of the most terrifying events in all of Scripture. In what is known as the "Great White Throne Judgment," every lost person from every generation throughout all of history is dragged into court. There they will receive a speedy and public trial, and then they will be sentenced for the crimes they've committed against their Creator.

In v. 11, we see that Someone is sitting on a great white throne, and the current heaven and earth are being destroyed at this time. As for who it is that's on the throne, we find that this is God the Son. If you read John 5:22-30; Acts 17:30-31; Rev. 21:5-6, you'll see that it's Jesus who occupies that seat. Jesus is the One the unbelieving world has rejected, and it will be Jesus who passes judgment upon them for their unbelief. As for the location of this terrible event, here's what David Jeremiah writes in his study Bible about the fact that "the earth and the heaven fled away": "The white throne is not set on the earth, because the earth is gone (II Pet. 3:10-13). Neither is it set up in what is commonly called heaven, because sinners are not allowed there. This judgment must then take place in some intermediate location between heaven and where the earth once was."[1]

I don't know if I agree with all of what Jeremiah says here, since Satan and many of his demons have access to heaven (Rev. 12:7-9) until they lose the battle against Michael and the righteous angels midway through the Tribulation. However, I do agree that no *human* unbeliever has ever darkened heaven's doorstep. Furthermore, I think Jeremiah's right in that v. 11 is telling us that the current heaven and earth will be destroyed at the time of this judgment of the lost.

Turn back to our text in Revelation 20 and look again at vs. 12-15. The sea, Death, and Hades, the abodes of all of history's lost people who've ever lived and died, will cough up their occupants and they will ALL stand before God the Son to face their judgment. Before we go any further, I want to turn to another of the most frightening passages of the Bible. Way back at the beginning of the New Testament, we read these words from the lips of our Lord: "Enter by the narrow gate; for wide is the gate and broad is the way that leads to destruction, and there are many who go in by it. Because narrow is the gate and difficult is the way which leads to life, and there are few who find it. Not everyone who says to Me, 'Lord, Lord,' shall enter the kingdom of heaven, but he who does the will of My Father in heaven. Many will say to Me in that day, 'Lord, lord, have we not prophesied in Your name, cast out demons in Your name, and done many wonders in Your name?' And then I will declare to them, 'I never knew you; depart from Me, you who practice lawlessness!'" (Matt. 7:13-14, 21-23).

I believe that these words are more frightening to me than anything I've ever heard, with only one exception: Rev. 20:11-15. Jesus Himself says that the way to life is the road with the fewest number of people on it. In other words, the vast majority of people will go to eternal doom, not bliss.

As if that weren't bad enough, Jesus goes on to say that there are a lot of people who will be deceived into believing they're going to heaven, only to discover too late that they've been wrong all along. Notice what it says in Matt. 7:22. These misguided people will try and read the Lord their resume, reminding Him of all the mighty works they did for Him. Now take this information in Matthew back to Rev. 20:11-15 and read the passage again. The last thing any of us should ever want from God is justice; what we want from God is mercy. But when people say that they believe they're going to heaven "because I'm a good person," in essence they're saying the words "Lord, Lord!"

No one standing at the Great White Throne is saved. Every single one of these people is lost, having been taken from their jail cells just long enough to have a few miserable seconds in court, with no attorney and no friends. These are people who traveled the broad road all their lives and failed to take the last exit ramp to the narrow road at the end of their time on earth. They will be in court, and they'll stand there all alone to face their accuser. There will be a Judge but no jury. There will be a Prosecutor but no one for the defense. There will be a trial but no waiting for a verdict. There will be a sentence, but there will be no appeal.

People who want to be judged based on their own merits will get exactly what they want. They will get the justice they demanded. They will receive not what they need, but what they deserve. They will, by their very own words and deeds, have played back for them in the sound of their hearing and in the sight of their eyes everything they've ever said and done, all recorded in "the books." What they will not hear is their name, which would have been recorded in the Lamb's Book of Life. And they, just like the devil, the Antichrist, and the False Prophet, will be thrown into the lake of fire, in a flame that is never quenched and where their suffering and torment will never end.

Now that you've heard the bad news, it's time for some good news. And it's on its way, for behold, our God makes all things new!

Chapter 30

Global Warming

In Rev. 21:1-8, we are given a foretaste of glory divine. John writes of a new heaven and earth, as the universe we now occupy is going to be replaced. He then peels back the curtain on the capital, the New Jerusalem. He compares this magnificent city to the beauty of a bride on her wedding day. But before John goes any deeper on the subject, he turns a corner on us. As important as it is for us to know about our permanent and indestructible home, it is far greater for us to read that our God will dwell among us. He will take away every last vestige of our sadness, as we will never again experience death or anguish of any kind! This section ends, though, with a warning. John provides a list of those who will *not* be with God and His elect. He writes that "...the cowardly, unbelieving, abominable, murderers, sexually immoral, sorcerers, idolaters, and all liars shall have their part in the lake which burns with fire and brimstone, which is the second death'" (Rev. 21:8).

I'll be coming back to this verse, but I want to go back to the subject of the new universe for a moment. It has been argued by some theologians in recent years that God will *refurbish* heaven and earth rather than *replace* them. They contend that if God is forced to destroy the current universe, this will give some kind of victory to Satan.

I have three responses to this assumption. First, that's an awfully hollow victory for Satan, since he'll be busy for the rest of eternity suffering far more than anyone will ever suffer. He's not going to be able to enjoy any kind of win over God, since he'll be "tormented day and night forever and ever." Second, it's time for another pop quiz. What is the most important thing in all of God's creation? Man! There are three things, in addition to the Godhead, that are going to last forever: God's Word, angels, and man. God gave man His Word in order that He might draw us to Himself (John 20:30-31). He gave us angels to protect us and minister to us (Heb. 1:13-14). And He sent us His Son to die for our sins and thereby purchase our redemption (II Cor. 5:21; I Pet. 3:18). Redeemed man is destined for glory and honor above all things (except for God Himself, of course – cf. Heb. 2:5-9). With man being that important, and considering how a vast majority of humanity will end up in the lake of fire, if there were any victory to be had by Satan it would be in all the condemned souls rather than by a destroyed universe.

Last but not least, go back to Revelation 21 and look again at the phrase "passed away" in v. 1. That's the Greek word "aperchomai", and it transliterates perfectly into the English; it means "passed away." The argument against a new universe says that "passed away" here suggests a restoration rather than a recreation, but there's a problem with that interpretation. Skip down and look at v. 4 again: "And God will wipe away every tear from their eyes; there shall be no more death, nor sorrow, nor crying. There will be no more pain, for the former things have *passed away*" (emphasis mine). There it is again, the "aperchomai." God says that death, sorrow, crying and pain will all be a thing of such a distant past that it will be as though they've never existed. They will all be gone. Consider the words of the Lord as recorded in the Old Testament: "For behold, I create new heavens and a new earth; And the former shall not be remembered or come to mind" (Isa. 65:17).

I see only one possibility here, and that is the complete and total destruction of the present universe. As if the evidence presented so far weren't persuasive enough, there's also a matter of what the apostle Peter has to say about it. In II Pet. 3:10-13, he reveals God's plan to destroy the universe. He even goes into a little bit of detail, explaining that the heavens will "pass away" (there's that phrase again), and everything – all the way down to the elements on the periodic table – will go up in smoke. He uses colorful words like "melt," "burned up," and "dissolved" to describe the scene. Read these verses for yourself; it should clear up every shred of confusion the issue could present. The present universe, which was created in six days, will be destroyed and replaced in an instant.

Not to keep piling on, but I would be remiss if I failed to address the word "create" in Isa. 65:17. It's the exact same Hebrew word used in the very first verse of the Bible, where it says that "In the beginning God created the heavens and the earth." What God did in creating the universe the first time, He will do again; it will be new, not refurbished!

I want to make one more passing comment about this topic. We're talking here about the destruction of the universe. There are quite a few people in the world right now who are busying themselves with the ostensibly noble task of saving the planet. I suppose that most of these folks have their hearts in the right place, but their fears are completely unfounded. Consider the promise of God to Noah. In Genesis 9:9-17, right after the Flood, God makes an unconditional covenant. God promises to Noah and every single descendant of his (which would include you and me!) that He will never again destroy the earth with water. In fact, God goes so far as to include every creature of the animal kingdom in the making of this covenant! The Lord concludes by telling Noah that He has set a rainbow in the sky to act as His signature of this promise. God is deadly serious when He says that there will be NO global flood ever again!

Either God is right or the Environmental Protection Agency is right. I'm going with God; you and I are <u>not</u> going to destroy this world. Oh, you can bet that there's coming a day of "global warming," but we are powerless to do anything to stop it. I wrote an essay somewhere around 2009, and it addressed the folly and gaping holes in the theory of Darwinian evolution. I want to quote from a section of that paper, as I believe it may help set the record straight when it comes to the litany of misinterpretations and misstatements being thrust upon the world by secular science. Naturalistic thinking has perched itself atop the horns of a dilemma, as their philosophy states on the one hand that mankind is obligated to take care of the planet, although at the same time they tell us that we are no more important than a blackjack tree or a stinkbug or a Siamese cat or a mongoose or a sponge or a barnacle. Here's what I wrote in response to this contradictory thinking:

> If naturalists are right, then everything in the universe is moving from a state of disorder toward a state of order, or at least from a state of order toward a state of even higher order. How, then, can an evolutionist say that there's a need for energy conservation or for environmentalism? If matter plus time plus chance is how everything came into being, if life sprang from nonlife, if the passage of time brings about greater order and complexity, then that means that it doesn't make any difference what man does to this planet. The material universe is, as Carl Sagan put it, "eternal" (all that will ever be). If naturalists are right, then life and creation are subject to the whims of Mother Nature, and man has no legitimate claim over the continuation of the planet anyway. (After all, the universe has successfully existed and grown into all its splendor over the course of billions of years without mankind raising one finger to help it.) I'll ask the question again: Since nature is in control of itself, and since everything including the human race is all here by some accident, what difference does it make what man does to conserve or recycle? We're just a transitional form, waiting to become something better, right? Whatever befalls our sacred world, we'll adapt and change to survive, right? Earth has a way of vomiting out the weak and unfit, right? We're not "stewards" of creation; we got here

by chance, so we're in subjection to it! How can the creature ever surpass its creator? If you're a naturalist, you can't say that man is responsible for creation: it started without man, it improved without man, it now exists with man as a mere transitional form, and one day it will exist with something greater than man. Man started as nothing and got here by accident. When a man dies, he merely ceases to exist. On some fine future day, man will be extinct and something better will replace us. So, pray tell, why am I supposed to save a planet that didn't want me here in the first place, will shortly expel me like a flea off a dog, and replace me and my kind with something better?[1]

My point here is simple. Either humanity is an accident of nature, which means that we have no stake in the future of our universe, OR God created man in His image and gave us this universe in order that we might have a place to worship and serve Him. Don't sweat this, my friend. God most assuredly will one day put an end to everything we now see. It is God *alone* who will do it, though, and with no help whatsoever from any of us. The destruction of this universe and its replacement will take place at the end of the Millennium, and it is the singular event that will bridge the gap between seven thousand years of history and eternity.

Chapter 31

We Shall Overcome

Going back to Rev. 21:1-8, there are a couple more things I'd like to explore. There's a curious observation that John makes about this new universe, and he states it in v. 1. He says that our new home will have "no more sea." There are at least three things that this "sea" can potentially represent. The first possibility is that it could be, well, a "sea," as in a gigantic body of water. Second, it can also refer to the world of politics. As we saw a while back, the Antichrist rises up out of the "sea" (Rev. 13:1) and becomes a political leader. There's also a reference to this idea back in the Old Testament. Read Dan. 7:1-8, paying special attention to vs. 2-3, and you will find there another description of the sea being the incubator for the political arena.

But there's also a third possible meaning to this "sea" that suddenly becomes extinct in our new environs. I Kings 6 and 7 describe the new temple that Solomon builds. In 7:23-26, there is a short list given of what the "sea" looks like. That "sea" is where the priests had to wash before they entered into God's presence. Why did God require the priests to bathe themselves as part of the sacrifice ritual? I believe the answer is found in Micah 7:19, where the prophet writes that God "...will cast all our sins into the depths of the sea." Have you ever heard the term "wash away your sins"? Of course you have! There's that gospel song, "What can wash away my sin? Nothing but the blood of Jesus!" There are several verses in the New Testament that give us those very words (cf. Acts 22:16; I Cor. 6:11; Tit. 3:5; Heb. 10:22).

Why is there not going to be a sea in the new heaven and earth? I certainly don't pretend to know all the answers to that question, but my first set of guesses would include the predictions that there will be no political jockeying and wrangling, and our sins will have been washed away in the sea of God's forgetfulness. Those sins will be buried in the bottom of the sea, and then that sea will be left completely out of our eternal home. How far does God separate us from our sins? As far as the east is from the west (Psa. 103:12)!

Okay, let's move on, gathering another nugget of truth from our text in Revelation 21. To refresh your memory, read vs. 5-8 again. In v. 7, the "overcomers" are promised an inheritance of all things, which includes the greatest thing, God Himself. Read Rom. 8:16-17; Gal. 3:26-29; Jas. 2:5. These overcomers are heirs with Christ, heirs of the new universe and heirs of Almighty God.

The question we have to answer now, though, is "What constitutes an 'overcomer'?" No need to speculate, as John explicitly defines the term for us: "For whatever is born of God overcomes the world. And this is the victory that has overcome the world – our faith. Who is he who overcomes the world, but he who believes that Jesus is the Son of God?" (I John 5:4-5). An overcomer, then, is someone who has Jesus, the Son of God, as his Savior.

The Bible then makes a contrast between the heirs of the Kingdom (the "overcomers") and those who will be left out in the cold (or *heat*, I guess I should say). In v. 8, there's a lengthy list of about eight different kinds of people who will suffer forever in the lake of fire. I can certainly see some of these characteristics in myself, especially when you understand these terms the way the Bible defines them. I've been known to be cowardly, abominable, unbelieving, and idolatrous on many more occasions than just a time or two. I have been immoral in just about every way the Bible describes immorality.

Does that mean I'm going to be excluded from heaven? Nope. Just remember who an "overcomer" is, and you'll be reminded of everything an overcomer actually overcomes, which is <u>all</u> of his sins, no matter how bad they are or how many times they've been committed. But what about that last trait of a lost man, where it says "all liars"? How many lies must someone tell in his life before he can legitimately be called a liar? Just one! If you've ever told a lie in your life, you're a liar. I've never met anyone who's never lied before (except for infants, of course). I remember once hearing a preacher say in a sermon that he'd never lied in his life, and he was in his seventies when he said it. I wanted to stand up in the middle of the sanctuary and cry out, "Sir, that's at the very least the second lie of your life!"

I can promise you that it hasn't been very long since I told my last lie. It probably won't be too awfully long before I tell my next one. So what are sinners like you and me to do about this problem? How do we deal with such a hopeless case? Well, there are a couple of things. First, if you're an "overcomer," then you've overcome *all* of your sins. Second, let's define the term "liar" in the context that it's presented here. Since John is the human author of Revelation, and since John has written about liars and lying in other biblical writings that bear his name, it seems appropriate to appeal to those other portions of Scripture in our quest for illumination on the subject.

Let me refer you to several places in John's first epistle. (By the way, it seems to be well beyond coincidence that I John speaks of both "overcomers" and "liars," just as our passage in Revelation does.) In I John 1:10, the apostle tells us that if we say we've never sinned, we are calling God a *liar*. In 2:4, you are a *liar* if you say that you know God but refuse to keep His commandments. Anyone who denies that Jesus is the Christ is a *liar*, and such a one is an antichrist (2:22). No one can say that they love God while at the same time harboring hatred for his brother. A man who is guilty of this sin is also a *liar* (4:20). And in 5:10, someone who doesn't believe God and His testimony about His Son is likewise a *liar*.

According to these passages, a "liar" is someone who possesses the following characteristics: (1) He denies his own sinfulness; (2) He refuses to keep God's commands; (3) he denies that Jesus is the Messiah, the Christ of God; (4) he hates his brother; and (5) He disbelieves the testimony of the Father about His Son.

I don't know about you, but that makes me feel a lot better. I am, after all, a liar in the way the world defines the word "lie." But this is a very specific definition that John gives us about who a liar is. The list I just gave you fits the description of the average unsaved man. If you're a child of God, you are *not* a "liar." However, if you don't have saving faith on the Lord Jesus, you *are* a "liar." If you fit into this classification, I urge you with all solemnity to come to the Savior. I promise you that if you cry out to the Lord Jesus, He will take you as His own and He <u>will</u> save you from your sins! No matter what you've done or for how long you've done it, He will not refuse you the ultimate gift, the free gift of salvation (John 6:37). If you don't remember anything else in this book, please remember this one thing. Either Jesus died for ALL of your sins, or He died for NONE of them; there is no middle ground.

James gives us sobering words about our brief time upon this earth. He writes: "Come now, you who say, 'Today or tomorrow we will go to such and such a city, spend a year there, buy and sell, and make profit'; whereas you do not know what will happen tomorrow. For what is your life? It is even a vapor that appears for a little time and then vanishes away" (Jas. 4:13-14). My friend, it makes no difference what your age or your state of health is. You have no guarantee that you'll still be alive in the next ten minutes. Come to the Lord Jesus, right this second, without delay. II Cor. 5:21 says that God "...made Him who knew no sin to be sin for us, that we might become the righteousness of God in Him."

You cannot rely on your own righteousness to get you anywhere with a perfect and holy God. You MUST trust in the perfect righteousness, the perfect sinlessness, and the sacrificial death of Jesus on the cross to be your payment for your sins. It is the ONLY way to heaven. In Rom. 10:9-10 (emphasis mine), Paul tells us that "...If you confess with your mouth the Lord Jesus and believe in your heart that God has raised Him from the dead, *you will be saved.* For with the heart one believes unto righteousness, and with the mouth confession is made unto salvation."

If you haven't taken the all-important step of receiving Jesus as your Savior and Lord, you can do it at this very moment. All you have to do is pray something like this: "God, I know that I'm a sinner. I have fallen short of the perfection that You expect of me. I know that my sin deserves judgment, but You promised to save me from my sin if only I would call upon You. I do that right now, Lord. Lord Jesus, I ask you to come into my heart and make it your permanent home. I trust You to forgive me and cleanse me of all my sins, and from this day forward I want you to be Lord and Master over my life. Thank You, Jesus, for saving me. Let me never be ashamed of You. I pray this in the Name of Jesus, Amen."

If you prayed a prayer like that just now, and if you truly meant that prayer with all your heart and with all your mind and with all your might, you now belong to God. He wants you to know that you can stand on this promise: if you want to go to heaven, all you have to do is trust in God's precious and perfect Son Jesus to take your sins away and replace them with His perfect righteousness. If you do that one thing, then I tell you on the authority of the Word of God that you WILL be saved!

Chapter 32

The New Jerusalem

Going back to our place in Revelation 21, we are given just a passing mention of the New Jerusalem (v. 2). It says there that John saw this sparkling city come down out of heaven as the centerpiece of the new earth. Keep reading, though, as much more is made of this glorious place in the verses that follow. Read verses 9-21. In verses 12-14, we're told that the city has twelve gates (three per side) and twelve foundations. Each gate represents a tribe of Israel, and each wall segment represents one of the twelve apostles. The city's inhabitants, then, will be people from both of these groups, the nation of Israel and the church.

Next, back up to vs. 9-10, and notice that the New Jerusalem is referred to as the bride of the Lamb. This, to me, is one of the strongest points for my case that the 24 elders (remember that discussion?) is representative of the two people groups on both sides of the cross. Since the city's perimeter is stamped with symbols of both OT and NT saints, the New Jerusalem will be occupied by both types of the redeemed, and the Scripture indicates that they are *all* called the "bride" of Christ.

Now I want to take a little time talking about the size of this magnificent city. Go back to v. 16, which reads: "The city is laid out as a square; its length is as great as its breadth. And he measured the city with the reed: twelve thousand furlongs. Its length, breadth, and height are equal." Please take special note here that the city is not a square, but a cube. Its length, breadth, and height are all equal in size. The NKJV says that the dimensions are twelve thousand "furlongs," but the Greek word is "stadia." A furlong is one-eighth of a mile, or 660 feet. A "stadion" (the singular form of "stadia"), however, is a little bit shorter, measuring only 606 feet. A "Roman mile" is eight times that figure, which is 4,848 feet, making it 432 feet shorter than our mile. So twelve thousand furlongs (or stadia) is about 1,377 miles, according to modern reckoning.

The question has been asked if the New Jerusalem will be big enough to hold all the saints of all the ages of time. I have two responses to that. First, the New Jerusalem is just the capital city of a new universe that can reasonably be expected to be as big as the present universe, so it doesn't really matter if everyone can fit in the city all at once. But second, let's do a little bit of math. Please don't balk; this is going to be a fun and rewarding exercise!

According to 2014 statistics, New York City is 305 square miles, and its current population is eight million, three hundred and thirty-seven thousand (8,337,000). That's a population density of 27,245 people per square mile. Now let's compare these numbers with the New Jerusalem. The headquarters of New Earth will be 1,337 miles times 1,337 miles, or 1,787,569 square miles. If we use the population density of the city of New York, the New Jerusalem can hold 48,702,317,405 people! That's 48.7 *billion* glorified bodies in one amazing city!

But hold on here! The New Jerusalem is also 1,337 miles *high*, too! That means its actual dimensions will be 2,389,979,753 *cubic miles*! Using that same formula – the population density of 27,245 people per square mile – New Jerusalem will be able to accommodate 65,114,998,370,485 people! That's right, over 65 *trillion*! And before you ask, the answer is "yes," as in "Yes, we will be able to fly!" We'll fly away at the Rapture. We'll fly back on flying white horses at the Second Coming. We'll be able to travel anywhere we want in the New Heaven as well as on the New Earth!

Don't quit now; I'm not quite finished with our little statistical game. I tried to figure out how many people have ever lived in all of history. That's a tough assignment, so I had to take a few liberties and make a couple of assumptions. Taking into account the fact that the world before the Flood was a much more suitable environment for long life and prolific reproduction, it would seem reasonable that we can use recent birth statistics and apply them across all the eons of time and come up with a realistic estimate.

According to a source I found on the internet, there were roughly 131.4 million live births in the world in the calendar year 2013.[1] I multiplied that figure by six thousand years of time from Adam down to the present day, which means my best guess is that a total of about 788.4 billion people have lived between Eden and 2014. Since the New Jerusalem can easily accommodate more than 65 trillion people, that means that the holy city will be able to hold more than *eighty-two times* more people than have ever lived! I think we can safely say that the New Jerusalem is going to have no trouble being able to take care of all God's people.

All right, I want to make one more observation about the New Jerusalem. In Rev. 21:21, we see that each of the twelve gates is made of one single 1,377-mile high pearl. I have heard the suggestion that God chose to inlay those gates with pearl because of the way that pearls are formed. Just as the oyster must be wounded or irritated in order to make this precious stone, our Savior had to suffer to purchase our redemption. These gates will be an eternal reminder to us all of Christ's mortal wounds and the benefits we've realized as a result of them.

Okay, let's go on to the next section of Scripture. Read Rev. 21:22-27, and you will find there will be no temple in the New Jerusalem. That's because God the Father and God the Son are the temple! The text also says that the Father and the Lamb are also the source of all light, so there will be no need for the sun or moon. Remember that I John 1:5 states that "...God is light and in Him is no darkness at all." We will see God as He really is (I John 3:2), and we shall walk in His light.

Staying on the subject of light for a moment longer, John writes that all the redeemed of all the nations from all the ages will dwell with the light of God, but only those whose names are written in the Book of Life will be there. Just as it is with every good presentation of the gospel, there is also a warning. In these verses, we're given a caution that is like the one we saw back up in v. 8, where liars and the abominable will be excluded from the holy city.

Now take a closer look at v. 25. We are told in this verse that the gates of the city will always remain open throughout the day, but then it parenthetically states that there shall be no night. It's a rather strange statement to make, but I believe it can be explained by the Jewish practice of repeating things for emphasis (cf. Prov. 26:4-5; II Pet. 3:8). The idea being put across here is that the New Jerusalem will be completely safe throughout eternity because only the righteous will be on the inside while the wicked will all be forever kept away. I like what McGee says in his commentary about it: "It is nonsense to say that the gates will not be shut at night because there is no night. Therefore, he says they will not be shut by day. In other words, they are going to throw away the key because there will be no danger. In John's day, a walled city had gates for the purpose of protection. When the gate of a city was closed, it meant that an enemy was on the outside and that they were trying to keep him there."[2]

No enemy of God will ever penetrate that city. There will be no darkness, which is another way of saying that there will be no crime (cf. I Thess. 5:5-8). There will be no sin, because there will be no sinners. Speaking of which, that leads us to the matter of v. 27. If your name is written in the Lamb's Book of Life, then you will never defile anyone or anything, you will never cause an abomination, and you'll never be the cause of any lie. That's because there will be no sin of any kind in the New Heaven and Earth, and therefore there will be no sinner of any kind there, either!

Twenty-one chapters down, one to go. Let's look at Rev. 22:1-5. This final chapter of the Bible begins with a tour of the area around God's throne. There is a river, which is made up of the "water of life," and its source is the very throne of God. There's also a street, and in the middle of that street and on each side of the river of life stands the tree of life. The tree produces twelve different kinds of fruit; each kind will be yielded by the tree for one month and then replaced by another kind. John then makes a comment about the leaves of the tree, which are for the "healing of the nations." He follows this up with the joyful remarks that we will actually see our God face to face, that there will be no more curse, and that His name will be engraved in our foreheads. Finally, we read that we will reign with our God "forever and ever."

If I may, I'd like to offer a few thoughts about this glorious passage. On this earth, there's no such thing as 100% pure water. It makes no difference how many times you run it through that reverse osmosis process (whatever that is), there's still going to be impurities in it. But that's not true of this water! The water of life is pure, clear, and perfect. And it will remain that way forever and ever.

Finally, there's the tree of life, which was in Eden and will be in the New Jerusalem. Curiously, this tree is found not only in the middle of the street; it's also on both sides of the river. I have concluded that there are two possibilities here. Either this is going to be a really big tree, or it's not just a single tree. I'm leaning toward the latter. I'm guessing there will be a host of these trees of life, but regardless of whether there is one tree or many trees, they'll be changing their fruit twelve times a year. There will be no night, and there will be no need to count days or weeks or months or years or decades or centuries or millennia, because eternity is *forever*. Nevertheless, the tree of life will perpetually provide twelve different fruit flavors, and I'm sure we will love them all!

In eternity, there will be no necessity in our eating or drinking in order to stay alive, as death will no longer be a threat to us (Rev. 21:4). Even so, we will be able to eat and drink as much as we want, and I'm sure that the fruit and water will be more scrumptious than anything anyone has ever consumed on this side of heaven! It's worth noting that we'll be like Adam and Eve were before the Fall in that we'll be vegetarians (or should I say "fruitatarians"?). I believe there will be animals on the New Earth, for I see no reason why there wouldn't be. I should point out, though, that there will be no sacrifices and no consuming of meat because there will be no death. To summarize, we'll eat and drink for the sheer enjoyment of it, and all the while we "shall reign forever and ever" (v. 5).

This concludes our look at our new and permanent home. If you're ready, turn the page, and we'll briefly examine God's final instructions to us.

Chapter 33

His Reward is with Him

We move now to the next set of verses, Rev. 22:6-11. John is told by his angelic tour guide that what he has just seen and heard is completely true and trustworthy, and that all of these things shall indeed come to pass. John is reminded that the Lord shall come "quickly," and then the blessing from Chapter 1 is repeated: to read and understand Revelation's prophetic truths is to be truly blessed of God! When the angel finishes his speech, John falls at his feet to worship him.

I'll say more about this in a minute, but the angel immediately instructs John not to do that, and he reiterates the Lord's admonition in Matt. 4:10 that we are to worship God and Him only. Then the angel declares that the words of John's newly-received prophecy are not to be sealed up, for the time of its fulfillment is "at hand" (which simply means that it is the next thing on God's timetable).

As I mentioned a moment ago, v. 7 is a flashback of what Jesus told John in Rev. 1:3, that there is a blessing from God Himself for our reading and believing the words of this book. Then we're told once again (vs. 8-9) that our worship is reserved for God alone, that only He is worthy of our praise and adoration, and for us to give that praise to another is just as blasphemous as withholding our worship from Him.

Then, in v. 10, we're given the exciting news that unlike previous Old Testament prophecies (Dan. 8:26; 12:4-10), this prophetic word is not to be sealed up. That means that as the end draws near, these prophecies will begin to make more and more sense. (We truly are living in exciting times, are we not?) The last sentence in this passage, v. 11, is something of a tongue-twister in addition to being a mindbender. The angel says that the unjust, the filthy, and the unrighteous will stay in their filth and unrighteousness. Then he says the same will be true of the holy and the righteous. The way its worded makes it sound like a riddle, but all he's saying is that everyone who dies lost will stay lost eternally. Conversely, all who leave this earth having been saved by the blood of Jesus will remain saved forever.

This is the same kind of concept we see in Jesus' story about Lazarus and the rich man in Luke 16. (By the way, this is a true story; it is NOT a parable.) Lazarus has died and is in paradise with Abraham, whereas the rich man dies and finds himself in hell. In v. 24, the rich man begs Abraham to send Lazarus to him with just a single drop of water to lessen his suffering. But Abraham replies in v. 26 that his request cannot be met, as there is an impassable chasm fixed between heaven and hell and no one can cross from one side to the other. Heb. 9:27 tells us that there is no second chance after we die; our eternal destiny will be set and irreversible based solely on whether or not we put our complete trust in the Lord Jesus, and our decision to do so can only be made on this side of the grave!

Okay, let's go on to the next section. In Rev. 22:12-17, Jesus takes over for the angel and He gives John the refrain that He is coming quickly, and when He does come His reward will be with Him. Jesus then goes on to say that each and every saint will be rewarded according to his work. Next, He refers to His divinity, as He calls Himself the Alpha and the Omega, the Beginning and the End, the First and the Last, the Root and the Offspring of David, and the Bright and Morning Star. Jesus continues, and He tells John that those who keep God's commandments are blessed, and that they will be able to enter into the New Jerusalem and even partake of both the tree of life as well as the water of life. But, just as we saw a little bit ago, the unredeemed will have no part in either God or His grand city; they will be locked out.

The first thing we're told in these verses is that our Lord is "coming quickly." This word "quickly" is the Greek word "tachu", and it means "before long; quickly; soon afterward." He's coming before long, meaning not long after these things are to take place. Notice next that when Jesus does come, He's bringing His reward with Him.

What is His reward? My argument here would be that our rewards will take the form of crowns, crowns that we will have earned while in this life after we've been saved. My reasoning for this is because of what we saw in the throne room of heaven. We were told, back in Rev. 4:2-4, about God sitting on His throne and that there are 24 elders sitting on thrones nearby (no way we can forget our discussion on the elders!). Then, skipping down to Rev. 4:9-11, we see the worship of the elders and the fact that they throw down their crowns at the base of the throne of God.

The elders, representative of God's saints, lay their crowns at the feet of Jesus. But what exactly are these crowns? Well, there are several places in the New Testament that speak of crowns for believers being given to us as a reward for our faithfulness. There are also different reasons for the bestowal of crowns, so they also represent several different kinds of rewards. Below is a list of these types of rewards.

First, there is the "imperishable crown." According to I Cor. 9:24-27, the Lord will give this reward as a symbol of the eternality of our salvation. It is an emphatic confirmation of the doctrine of eternal security (what some denominations like to call "once saved, always saved"). The second type of crown, the "crown of rejoicing," is described in I Thess. 2:13-19. This crown represents our victory over persecution from Satan and evil men. Third is the crown of righteousness (II Tim. 4:8), followed by the crown of life (Jas. 1:12; Rev. 2:10). The crown of life is mentioned in conjunction with successfully enduring temptation and remaining faithful unto death.

There is also a fifth crown, which is apparently reserved for shepherds of God's flock. I Pet. 5:1-4 tells us about a "crown of glory," which will be conferred upon exemplary elders and pastors. For more information on our rewards and what these crowns mean, I recommend the outstanding book "Your Eternal Reward: Triumph and Tears at the Judgment Seat of Christ" by Erwin Lutzer.

I will go on record here as saying that whether we will keep our crowns or cast them at the Lord's feet is a matter of some debate. I am uncertain as to whether we will hang onto our crowns, although I tend to believe that we will. (The throwing of crowns before the throne in Rev. 4:10 may be a metaphor for giving all glory and honor back to the One who created and saved us.) I would hasten to add, though, that the actual duties and privileges that each of these crowns represents will last forever, throughout all eternity. Don't be afraid to get greedy for God's approval and rewards!

Go back to Rev. 22:16 now, and look at it again. Here we see the signature line for the Author of this book, and it's none other than Jesus Himself. Let's also revisit the list of names that the Lord attributes to Himself in vs. 13, 16. He calls Himself the Alpha and the Omega, the Beginning and the End, the First and the Last, the Root and the Offspring of David, and the Bright and Morning Star. Each of these names is found elsewhere in Scripture, and they speak of both the divinity and the humanity of Jesus.

Verses 14-15 remind us one last time that there are two, and only two, kinds of people in this world. There are the redeemed of God and there are the lost. (Or, as the late Adrian Rogers liked to say, there are only "saints and ain'ts.") Then, skipping down to v. 17, this is not an invitation from the church being given to men. Rather, it's a petition by the church pleading for her Lord to come!

Now comes one final hard shot of sober warning. Tampering with God's Word is something that comes at a heavy price. Read these words carefully. "You shall not add to the word which I command you, nor take from it, that you may keep the commandments of the Lord your God which I command you" (Deut. 4:2). "Whatever I command you, be careful to observe it; you shall not add to it nor take away from it" (Deut. 12:32). "Every word of God is pure; He is a shield to those who put their trust in Him. Do not add to His words, Lest He rebuke you, and you be found a liar" (Prov. 30:5-6).

Let me end this section with one vital parting thought. The Word of God is complete just as it's written. There is to be no adding to God's Word, and there is to be no taking away from it. The Bible is all the written revelation that we will ever receive from the Almighty. If there is something it says that you don't understand, do not fret or be intimidated. Simply ask God for wisdom according to the prescription of Jas. 1:5-8, then search the Scriptures to find your answer. Trust God to show you and teach you as much as He wants you to understand, work diligently to rightly divide the Word (II Tim. 2:15), and then simply lean on Him for the things He doesn't reveal to you (Prov. 3:5-6).

Always remember this: It's okay to be wrong, but once you've been shown through the Scripture that you're wrong, change your thinking to conform to the revealed Word of God (Rom. 12:2). Refusing to repent of thought or deed in the face of scriptural evidence to the contrary is a road that no one should ever desire to walk. Pride is perhaps the most lethal of all sins. Don't allow yourself to become puffed up about anything, lest your pride become an obstacle to a right relationship with your Father in heaven (in addition to becoming a hindrance to your spiritual growth).

I close Part 4 with the last two verses of the Bible, Rev. 22:20-21: "He who testifies to these things says, 'Surely I am coming quickly.' Amen. Even so, come, Lord Jesus! The grace of our Lord Jesus Christ be with you all. Amen."

Part Five

The Seventieth Week of Daniel

Chapter 34

Introduction to Daniel's Eschatology

As I stated way back in the preface, to understand Dan. 9:24-27 is to understand the rudiments of end-time prophecy. These four meaty verses create serious difficulties for every eschatological view other than the premillennial one. I believe that you will see many of these problems begin to take shape as you work your way through this final section of the book. By contrast, the view posited by this book is actually strengthened by a good and right understanding of these verses.

Everything I've written up to this point will hopefully answer some questions that may have been nagging at you, but I'm sure that in answering those questions, more will have come up. (Ain't it the way?) I saved this section for last because I think it may help you with both your older unresolved problems in addition to your newest ones.

The balance of our time together will be devoted almost exclusively to the aforementioned verses, but I want to prepare you now for the fact that this is a big task you're about to undertake. The Bible is the only book that God wrote, which automatically makes it the most beautiful thing ever written while at the same time being the most difficult to plumb. The basic message of God's Word is simple enough a child can understand it, yet the wisest of men have been striving to search its depths for as long as the Book has been around.

I submit to you that this passage we're about to study provides as many challenges as anything that has ever been written. If the going gets tough, just remember the words of Prov. 25:2: "It is the glory of God to conceal a matter, But the glory of kings is to search out a matter." Don't be afraid of the work ahead; I promise you that the reward shall be great!

Chapter 35

The Prayer that Brings the Prophecy

Before we get into the prophetic words given to Daniel by the angel Gabriel, I want to say a few words about the whole chapter first. What makes this a wonderful section of Scripture is the grandeur and beauty in which two great themes are put on display: prayer and prophecy. Daniel was a man who made prayer a top priority throughout his entire life. The petition he offers to God, found in Dan. 9:3-19, is the culmination of that prayer life. Daniel's entreaty is so filled with remorse for himself and his people over their sins against God that he actually gets interrupted by a well-known messenger from heaven. Look at the verses that follow, Dan. 9:20-22.

Daniel reports that right in the middle of his prayer of contrition, none other than the mighty angel Gabriel literally flies into Daniel's airspace and announces that he's going to give the prophet the ability to understand a message straight from the Lord. Isn't this incredible? Daniel's prayer was given personal, verbal attention from one of God's own emissaries. Not only is Gabriel appearing to Daniel here (for the second time, no less), he's also come with the news that Daniel is about to be given a unique and wonderful ability to understand something that no one else has ever been told.

This is a little sidelight here, but it's worth stopping at this scriptural turnout in order to be reminded of a fundamental principle. Let's back up just a few verses and look at one really outstanding sentence of Daniel's prayer; please read v. 13. Notice the sequence here, where Daniel says that "...we have not made our prayer before the Lord our God, that we might turn from our iniquities and understand Your truth." Please don't miss this. There are three distinct parts to this seemingly simple verse; I'm going to review them in reverse order. If you want to understand God's truth, you must first be cleansed of your sins. And if you desire to be cleansed of your sins, first you must pray.

Our salvation is couched in our faith, and our faith is rooted in prayer. Perhaps this is why we're given the admonition in I Thess. 5:17 to "pray without ceasing." When we pray, we are cleansed of our sins. Then, once we are restored to a right relationship with the Lord, we are better able to understand His truth. One of the big reasons why unsaved people can't identify with the Bible is because their sins haven't been forgiven (John 3:18). Their sins haven't been forgiven because they don't have saving faith. Without faith, it's impossible to please God (Heb. 11:6). They don't have a relationship with God, so they don't pray. Since the Bible has been rightly called "God's love letter to His children," the Scriptures are a hazy, unintelligible mystery to those who don't know Him.

Okay, let's go back to v. 22, and we'll see this concept in action. Thanks to Daniel's prayer, primarily because of its elements of contrition, he is given the very special blessing that he will be able to understand something that is about to be given exclusively to him. This brings us to the transition in this chapter from prayer to prophecy. Daniel's marvelous prayer results in God giving a prophetic vision, easily one of the most important prophecies in all of Scripture. Beginning with the next chapter, we'll read it and break it down together.

Chapter 36

An Overview of the Seventy Weeks

"'Seventy weeks are determined For your people and for your holy city, To finish the transgression, To make an end of sins, To make reconciliation for iniquity, To bring in everlasting righteousness, To seal up vision and prophecy, And to anoint the Most Holy. Know therefore and understand, That from the going forth of the command To restore and build Jerusalem Until Messiah the Prince, There shall be seven weeks and sixty-two weeks; The street shall be built again, and the wall, Even in troublesome times. And after the sixty-two weeks Messiah shall be cut off, but not for Himself; And the people of the prince who is to come Shall destroy the city and the sanctuary. The end of it shall be with a flood, And till the end of the war desolations are determined. Then he shall confirm a covenant with many for one week; But in the middle of the week He shall bring an end to sacrifice and offering. And on the wing of abominations shall be one who makes desolate, Even until the consummation, which is determined, Is poured out on the desolate'" (Dan. 9:24-27).

That's quite a mouthful, huh? Well, we're going to make sense of it by breaking it down into bite-size pieces. We'll start by separating it one verse at a time, and then we shall tackle each verse, one line at a time. Verse 24 gives the prophecy as a summary statement, both in terms of the timing of the prophecy as well as the most significant highlights of it. Then, v. 25 explains the signs to look for in the first sixty-nine weeks. Verse 26 follows it up with a proclamation of the climax and conclusion of those sixty-nine weeks. Finally, v. 27 wraps everything up with the highlights of the seventieth and final week, including the timing of when it will begin.

We'll begin by going back to v. 24, and we will tear it down piece by piece, line by line, and phrase by phrase. The first phrase we encounter is two little words, "seventy weeks." If you go all the way back to Chapter 3 of this book, you can refresh yourself on how we know how much time seventy weeks represents (490 years) and how we arrive at that. The first sixty-nine weeks, or 483 years, have already elapsed. There are three major events outlined in this portion of the prophecy. First, there was the order for Jerusalem to be rebuilt. Second, the people moved back from captivity and carried out these orders to rebuild. And third, the Messiah came to His people, but they had Him murdered (or, as Daniel put it, He was "cut off").

But there still remains one more "seven" (or "week") that has been set aside for Daniel's people and their holy city. We'll look at that phrase "...for your people and for your holy city" in a little bit, but there are two more words that are sandwiched in between this phrase and the introductory words "seventy weeks." Do you see those two words? They're the words "are determined." In Acts 1:7, Jesus tells the disciples as He's ascending into heaven that God has fixed, or *determined*, the time of His return. This is in perfect keeping with what was revealed to Daniel. Jesus was simply repeating what Daniel was initially told, that God the Father has set a time for the Son's return, which is what Daniel's prophecy climaxes with, the Second Coming! That time was set in eternity past, and nothing will change it.

The last portion of that first phrase in Dan. 9:24 says that the seventy weeks have been determined "...for your people and for your holy city." This should be an easy one to figure out! Now remember, the angel Gabriel is speaking, but who is his audience? Daniel, of course! Hence, when he speaks of "your" people and "your" holy city, he's talking about Daniel's people and Daniel's holy city. That can only be a reference to one people group, i.e. the Jews, and only one city, Jerusalem. All we're doing here is making some building blocks as we go, so this would be a good summary of v. 24: "490 years are fixed for the Jews and Jerusalem."

All right, let's move on to the second phrase. This is the first of six rapid-fire, staccato phrases that act like Muhammad Ali. You know, "Dance like a butterfly, sting like a bee!" Just pow-pow-pow-pow!! Each is a separate prophetic utterance, and collectively they comprise the highlights of this 490-year stretch of time. Imagine taking any five consecutive centuries throughout history and summing up their most important events in only six little phrases. Well, that's exactly what God does here. Talk about an economy with words! When God speaks like this, wasting no breath, we want to walk very carefully but drill deep to mine this vital passage.

The opening phrase says: "To finish the transgression." Gabriel's choice of words here reminds me of what Paul wrote in II Thess. 2:9-12: "The coming of the lawless one is according to the working of Satan, with all power, signs, and lying wonders, and with all unrighteous deception among those who perish, because they did not receive the love of the truth, that they might be saved. And for this reason God will send them strong delusion, that they should believe the lie, that they all may be condemned who did not believe the truth but had pleasure in unrighteousness."

Do you see what I see? Notice back in Daniel that the phrase is "<u>the</u> transgression", with the definite article. Here in II Thessalonians, it says in v. 11 that those who are perishing will believe <u>the</u> lie. That would be the lie that Satan told Eve in the Garden, the lie that she could be like God. It's the same lie that Satan has peddled to the whole human race ever since. But back to "<u>the</u> transgression," it's as though God expects us to know what He's talking about, since there's only <u>one</u> transgression. In order to unearth this bit of truth, let's glance back at what we've learned so far. This prophecy, as we just saw in the opening phrase, is directed specifically at the Jews. That means we're narrowing the "transgressors" significantly, because the transgression, whatever it is, was committed by the Jews.

It just so happens that these words refer back only a few verses, because Daniel actually mentioned this "transgression" in his prayer that brought the whole world this great prophecy. Go back just a short distance and read vs. 8-11. In v. 11, Daniel says that "...all Israel has *transgressed* God's law, and has departed so as not to obey [His] voice." That's a big, general, all-encompassing confession of sin, but it is Israel's sin, which is her disobedience to God's law. As a result, somewhere in this period of 490 years, God is going to bring an end to Israel's sin of disobedience.

One down, five to go. The next phrase says this: "To make an end of sins." I see a little paradox in this phrase. Let me show you what I mean. In Heb. 9:24-26, we learn that Jesus offered Himself as a sacrifice that went straight into the presence of the Father. These verses make clear that Jesus' sacrifice was unlike the kind the Jewish priests had to make, because they had to perform their sacrifices over and over again. Jesus, however, paid the full price for our sins by laying down His own perfect, sinless life. The wording of v. 26 is that in this transition from the blood of animals to the blood of the Savior, Jesus accomplished the once-for-all-time task of having "put away sin." It's obvious that whatever is meant by "putting away sin," it doesn't mean that no one sins any more, since *everyone* still sins! You know what that means, don't you? It's the Law of Double Fulfillment, called back into action!

Actually, there's a significant amount of this prophecy we're studying that falls into that classification. Let your memory take you back to Chapter 3, where I first introduced the Law of Double Fulfillment into our discussion. You will recall that all this law says is that a Bible prophecy will be fulfilled twice, the first time in part and the second time in full. This happens a lot more often than one might think. Earlier, I used Jesus' mention of the destruction of the temple in Matthew 24 as an example of this law, and I also used Luke 4:16-21 and the subtle way in which the Lord told the congregants at the synagogue that there would be two advents. We touched on this subject back in Chapter 26, but I want to add a couple more thoughts about it here.

Jesus Himself, in Luke 4:21, tells the people that he is the fulfillment of the Scripture He just read, which is found in Isa. 61:1-2. This is actually the start of a really long section of Isaiah that gives us a litany of details about the coming Millennium (some of which we have already covered), but what I want you to see is in v. 2: "To proclaim the acceptable year of the Lord..." As soon as He uttered those words, Jesus stopped abruptly, literally in mid-sentence, handed the scroll of Isaiah back to the attendant, and plopped Himself down. Then He told His hearers that He was the fulfillment of all that He'd just read.

But guess what? There's coming a day when He's going to fulfill the rest of the prophecy, starting with the very next phrase here in v. 2: "And the day of vengeance of our God..." Jesus, by His own words here, shows us how the Law of Double Fulfillment works. He fulfilled part of the prophecy in the Incarnation (His first coming), and He'll finish the job when He returns.

The same holds true for the prophetic phrase we're looking at. Jesus took away the *penalty* of our sins in His first coming when He died on the cross, and then one day yet future He's going to obliterate the *presence* of sins when He returns and sets up the Millennial Kingdom. When it comes to the phrase "to make an end of sins," we must maintain our focus. We need to remember the cause of these events, which is the Messiah, and we also have to keep in mind the object of the action, that being the children of Israel. Therefore, when the Scripture says that there will be an end of sins, it means that namely the sins of *Israel* will be brought to an end. Israel is up to her eyeballs in sin today, is she not? "How so?" you might ask. Because of her rejection of her Messiah!

However, when Messiah returns, Israel will repent and be saved. The prophet Zechariah tells us how that will happen, in Zech. 12:7-10. These verses are explicit in the exalted place of the nation of Israel, the tribe of Judah in particular. God reveals that Judah will be saved first so that he shall not be looked upon with contempt by his brethren. In fact, the glory of Judah will ultimately excel them all.

The passage goes on to say that in the day of Israel's salvation, even the weakest among the people will be as strong as mighty warrior David, and the house of David will have the strength of God. When that happens, God will destroy all the nations that have come against Jerusalem. In turn, the children of Israel shall be saved, as they will truly see their Messiah for who He is and they will mourn over their rejection of Him. This is the script for the opening act of the Millennium, when Jesus returns with His saints at the Second Coming.

Verses 7-8 tell of the Lord's interrupting the festivities of Armageddon (cf. v. 11) by bringing salvation to His people Israel. In v. 9, Jesus will begin the weeding-out process in strong fashion by stamping out the nations of the world who've come to do battle against His chosen people. Then, in v. 10, the children of Israel will grieve over their sin of having killed their King. However, the story doesn't end with a *sad* Israel. It ends with a *saved* Israel. Just keep reading: start with v. 11 and read down through 13:1. Notice in v. 1 that it says that a "fountain" shall be opened. That is a reference to Jesus' atoning work on the cross (see Psa. 36:9; Jer. 2:13; 17:13; Rev. 21:6). That fountain, who is Jesus our

Lord, will be opened to the nation of Israel as her Redeemer, and He will purify her of her sin. In simple terms, this phrase means that the Lord will put an end to Israel's sin when He removes His people's veil and they look upon Him and accept Him as Messiah and King.

Chapter 37

On Earth as it is in Heaven

Continuing on, let's return to Dan. 9:24 and look at the next phrase: "...to make reconciliation for iniquity..." So far, we've seen that the presence of sin on earth will come to an end at the Parousia (which is what's meant by the term "finish the transgression"). We've seen that Israel's sin in particular will be wiped out. Now we are given this expression, which adds a new feature. Do you see it? In each of these first three phrases, a different word is used in describing acts of rebellion against God: transgression, sin, and iniquity. The first two phrases speak of a cessation of sin ("finish," "end"), while this third phrase changes the subject from "ending" sin to "reconciling" it.

Now we've hit on something pretty important. Let's look at this new word, "reconciliation." It's the Hebrew word "kaw-phar'", and it means "appease, make atonement, cleanse, disannul, forgive, be merciful, pacify, pardon, purge, reconcile." It's the same word that's found in a most unlikely verse. Turn back to Genesis 6, where God is telling Noah how to build a boat. In vs. 13-14, we read that God prepares Noah for what He is about to do, which is to destroy the world with water. He instructs Noah to build an ark out of gopherwood, and he is to cover the ark both inside and outside with pitch, which will waterproof the wood. That word "pitch" is the exact same word in Daniel, "kawphar." Noah had to put a barrier between the ark (the vessel of salvation) and the water (the emblem of God's wrath).

What it all boils down to here is that the word "reconciliation" actually refers to our being protected against God's righteous anger toward us. That makes this word a perfect synonym for another theological term, "propitiation." This word carries some heavy doctrinal weight, so it is wise for you to know what it means. Take a hard right back to the other end of your Bible and read I John 2:2; 4:10. Jesus Himself is the "propitiation" for our sins. He is the "reconciliation" between evil mankind and a holy God. In Rom. 3:21-25, we read this (emphasis mine): "But now the righteousness of God apart from the law is revealed, being witnessed by the Law and the Prophets, even the righteousness of God, through faith in Jesus Christ, to all and on all who believe. For there is no difference; for all have sinned and fall short of the glory of God, being justified freely by His grace through the redemption that is in Christ Jesus, whom God set forth as a *propitiation* by His blood, through faith, to demonstrate His righteousness, because in His forbearance God had passed over the sins that were previously committed..."

Do you see there in v. 25, where it says that God provided a propitiation (aka "reconciliation") "by His *blood*"? I always cringe a little when I hear someone say that they "gave their heart to Jesus" or they "took Jesus into their heart" or they "received Jesus." Even Muslims and Buddhists will tip their hat to Jesus, but that doesn't save anybody. In the same way Noah desperately needed a waterproofing agent that would protect him from God's wrath, you and I need something that will protect us. That's where the blood of the Savior comes in. When I say that I tend to grimace over someone "giving their heart to Jesus," it's because Jesus doesn't want your heart. Seriously, what does a perfect and holy God want with that rotting, putrid thing? No! He wants to give you a *new* heart (cf. Ezek. 36:26).

Read Rom. 5:9; Eph. 2:13; I John 1:7. Rom. 5:9 explains that Jesus' *blood* justifies us and keeps us from wrath (just like the pitch on the ark!). Eph. 2:13 says that we're brought near to God by the *blood* of His Son. And in I John 1:7, we see that it is Jesus' *blood* that washes our sins away. (See also Heb. 9:12-14, which stresses the importance of Jesus having shed His blood for our sins.)

All this is to say that Jesus is going to "finish the transgression" when He returns to set up His kingdom. He will "make an end of sins" when He removes the veil from Israel's eyes, and then they'll see Him as their Messiah. And now, Jesus will have made "reconciliation for iniquity" by purchasing His children with the protective covering of His blood. This third phrase – this third prophecy – took place at the cross, at the end of the 69 weeks. The first two prophecies won't come to pass until the end of the Seventieth Week, which will be Armageddon and the Parousia. Okay, on to the next phrase. Back in our verse, Dan. 9:24, the next prophecy mentioned is "...to bring in everlasting righteousness..." Let's look at a few verses that will help us better understand this. We'll go first to Jer. 23:5-8: "'Behold, the days are coming,' says the

Lord, 'That I will raise to David a Branch of righteousness; A King shall reign and prosper, And execute judgment and righteousness in the earth. In His days Judah will be saved, And Israel will dwell safely; Now this is His name by which He will be called: THE LORD OUR RIGHTEOUSNESS. Therefore, behold, the days are coming,' says the Lord, 'that they shall no longer say, 'As the Lord lives who brought up the children of Israel from the land of Egypt,' but, 'As the Lord lives who brought up and led the descendants of the house of Israel from the north country and from all the countries where I had driven them.' And they shall dwell in their own land.'"

The Bible is loaded with passages that make preterism a worthless doctrine, but these four verses are right near the top of the list. One big way we can know for sure the Bible's prophecies aren't completely fulfilled is the fact that Israel, though her people are back in their land, is not yet dwelling <u>safely</u> (v. 6).

But there is so much more that's crammed into these few verses. In v. 5, God says He'll raise up a King from the line of David who will bring pure justice and complete righteousness to the world. Verse 6 says that Israel and Judah (referring to the divided kingdom being brought together again – cf. Ezek. 37:15-28) will be together in the land under this one King, whose name is "The Lord our Righteousness." Then, vs. 7-8 make it clear that this will happen, not to the Israelites of old or even from the time of the OT prophets, but rather to their descendants who've been scattered all over the world and ultimately brought back to the land of Canaan.

If those first 3 phrases are the Himalayas of prophecy, then this fourth phrase (bringing in everlasting righteousness) is the Mt. Everest. To "bring in everlasting righteousness" is what we're taught to pray for in the Lord's Prayer ("Your kingdom come" – Matt. 6:10). It's what the disciples were looking for when their Messiah was ascending back into heaven (Acts 1:6-7). To bring in everlasting righteousness literally means to bring the Everlasting Righteous King to this earth to make it happen!

Chapter 38

The Sealing of Prophecy

It's time now to move on to the fifth phrase, "...to seal up vision and prophecy..." We should already know what is meant by the words "vision" and "prophecy," so the key to unlocking the mystery of this sequence is the word "seal." It's the Hebrew word "khaw-tham'" and it means "to close up or seal up, make an end, mark, stop." What this phrase is saying, then, is that prophecies and visions will come to a screeching halt.

Compare this to the use of that same word "seal" found only a couple of pages away. Read Dan. 12:4. Not only was the full meaning of the book of Daniel hidden from the man who wrote it, it was also hidden from the entire world "until the time of the end." If you want to know how close to the end we are, just read commentaries and books about Daniel that were written long ago and then compare them with how much we understand today. The reason that Dan. 9:24-27 is so important is because these four verses are the nucleus around which all of end-time prophecy spins.

Here's the main thrust of the phrase "to seal up vision and prophecy": if the predictions given in these verses are starting to come into focus, then the visions and prophecies are no longer sealed. Or, to put it another way, we can know whether or not all seventy weeks have passed if we're able to determine that all of the

the close of the Old Testament period) was forty-nine years, the "seven weeks."

That decree was issued in 445 B.C., so this takes us to about 396 B.C. There was certainly a lot of opposition by Israel's enemies as they tried to rebuild, which is what's meant by the phrase "troublesome times." But the Jews prevailed, their detractors were vanquished, and Jerusalem once again was inhabited by God's chosen people.

This brings us to the remaining sixty-two weeks. The seven weeks (forty-nine years) refers to the length of time it would take after Artaxerxes' decree until the temple would be rebuilt. That leaves us with 434 years (sixty-two weeks), which refer to the time that would elapse between the finishing of the temple and the coming of Messiah. It really is worth repeating that the fulfillment of this seven-week prophecy and rebuilding of the temple coincides with the closing of the Old Testament period. The book of Malachi and Nehemiah 13 are the last of the Old Testament recordings, chronologically speaking, and the completion of Jerusalem and the temple also take place during this time.

This roughly 400 years of silence is often called the "Intertestamental Period." That silence was finally broken when Gabriel (yes, the same angel who appeared to Daniel) came along in Luke 1 and told Zacharias and Mary of the miraculous births in which they would play major roles (with John the Baptist and Jesus, respectively). Even though these so-called "400 years of silence" were marked by God's voice being conspicuously absent, there were prophecies that were fulfilled either in whole or in part during that time.

Of special interest are the prophecies found in Daniel 2, 7, 8, 11 that address the kingdoms of Babylon, Medo-Persia, Greece, and Rome that rose and fell during that 400-year epoch. God's silence was deafening during those four centuries, but we can look back and clearly see the work of His hands throughout that age. We observe the same kind of providential involvement from the closing of the New Testament canon (in ca. A.D. 95) down through this present hour. God has not spoken since He gave John the book of Revelation, but His plan has unfolded, often imperceptibly, one piece at a time ever since then.

As to the 62 weeks, a man named Sir Robert Anderson wrote a book entitled "The Coming Prince." According to Anderson's research, the period from Nisan 1 in 445 B.C. (Artaxerxes' decree) until Nisan 10 in A.D. 32 (Jesus' entry into Jerusalem on Palm Sunday) was exactly 173,880 days.[1] If you divide that number by 360 (the number of days in the Jewish year), you arrive at 483, the number of years *to the day* in the fulfilling of the 62-week portion of the prophecy. Isn't it amazing how the children of Israel, who had their Tanakh (the Jewish Old Testament) memorized, couldn't see that this Man riding on a donkey and entering the Old City to the cheers and worship of thousands, was the Messiah of whom Daniel wrote?

Chapter 40

Messiah is Cut Off

The wheels on the bus go round and round, so keep pressing on and read v. 26. The verse starts out by giving us the time frame "after the 62 weeks." As we just saw, the word "after" could just as easily be replaced with the phrase "at the conclusion of," because it's <u>exactly</u> at the end of the 69 weeks that our Lord is crucified. See, that's the action part of this prophecy. The second phrase is "Messiah will be cut off," with the back end of that phrase being one of two different renderings. Either the Messiah will be cut off (i.e. put to death) "...but not for himself" (NKJV, KJV), or He'll be cut off "...and have nothing" (ASV, AMP, CEV, ESV, HCSB, NASB, NIV, NLT, NRSV).

I want to spend a few minutes looking at this little phrase here. I'm not at all confused by the Messiah being cut off, which is a term repeatedly used throughout the Old Testament as a euphemism for "executed" or "put to death" (cf. Gen. 9:11; 17:14; Exo. 12:15, 19; 30:33). It's also pretty evident that the phrase "not for Himself," using simple deductive reasoning, means that the Messiah would die for someone else. Or, to put it another way, He would die in another man's place. That part is easily solved. But the vast majority of translations, which articulate the phrase as being that the Messiah will "have nothing," leave me scratching my head.

The first question we can ask ourselves is "Why the big difference in wording between two translations and all the others?" The answer is because some of those other translations came from different manuscripts than the KJV or NKJV did. What is meant, then, by the statement that the Messiah will die and "have nothing"? I looked in all my commentaries, and not a single one made a direct reference to the phrase. Nobody wanted to take a stab at it. Isn't that typical? You just can't get people to tackle the tough stuff (sigh). Not even the Treasury of Scripture Knowledge was helpful, and when that happens, you know you're on own!

But I did find a little something, and I want to share it with you in hopes that it may be of some help. Let me give you the passage as it reads in the Amplified Bible. It reads: "And after the 62 weeks [of years] shall the Anointed One be cut off or killed and shall have nothing [and no one] belonging to [and defending] Him." In other words, Messiah will die alone and basically friendless. That seems to be of some help, doesn't it? And how about the NLT? It puts it this way: "After this period of 62 sets of 7, the Anointed One will be killed, *appearing to have accomplished nothing...*" Oooohhh, I like that! That helps quite a bit, don't you think? Every last one of Jesus' disciples was filled with abject despondency after His death; they thought He was going to be the Redeemer of Israel, but He died and left all those prophecies yet unfulfilled (cf. Luke 24:19-21)!

All right, so Messiah will die alone, friendless, and seemingly without purpose, which is exactly how Jesus' death looked to the entire world for a couple of days. Still building, it's time to move on. Getting back to Dan. 9:26, let's look at the next phrase: "And the people of the prince who is to come shall destroy the city and the sanctuary." Now this section is a lot easier to untangle. The key to understanding this section is breaking it down into three parts: (1) The people; (2) The prince to come; and (3) The destruction of the city and the sanctuary. What we want to do is examine the third part first, because if we can figure out what is meant by "the city and the sanctuary," we can then determine who destroyed them. From there, it's a domino effect, as we'll then know who "the people" are and, in turn, where this "prince" will come from.

Let's see if we can figure out what city and what sanctuary we're talking about. We'll start by making a small assumption, that being that "the sanctuary" is in "the city." I believe that's a very safe assumption, as we already know that this entire prophecy revolves around Daniel's people and their holy city (v. 24). As we discussed earlier, that "holy city" can only be one place: Jerusalem. And, as it happens, that's where the "sanctuary" is, too, because the sanctuary is simply another name for the temple. How do we know that? Because for the Jew, there have been only two sanctuaries. Initially, it was the tabernacle in the wilderness, and then it was the temple in Jerusalem.

From the time Daniel's prophecy was written until this portion of it was fulfilled, over 500 years had elapsed.

This partial fulfillment came in A.D. 70 when General Titus and his Roman army marched on Jerusalem, besieged and sacked it, and *mostly* destroyed the Temple. (You may remember that we discussed this back in Chapter 3 in my explanation of the Law of Double Fulfillment.) There. We just now answered the first question, "Who are the people that destroyed the city and the sanctuary?" Answer: The Romans. The Romans are the object of this third part (i.e. the ones who destroyed the city and the sanctuary), which means that we have now answered the first part, too. The Romans are "the people" of "the prince who is to come." Now all we need to do is figure out who this "prince" might be.

Chapter 41

The Coming Flood

This prince, whoever he is, must be very important, because he is the focus of the remainder of the prophecy. Jump ahead for just a moment and read Dan. 9:27. It says that "he" will confirm a covenant and "he" will bring an end to sacrifice and offering. Obviously, this prince will be a very powerful figure. He'll broker some kind of treaty, or covenant, and he'll also attack the Jews in some way when he puts a stop to their sacrifices. Couple that information with the fact that he'll come from the Roman Empire, and you have a "prince" who is most definitely NOT the Messiah. The Messiah is a Jew, not a Roman. The Jews didn't destroy Jerusalem, but the Romans did. So whoever this prince is, he's Roman, and he's intent on doing harm to the children of Israel. We'll discuss more about this mysterious character in a little bit, but first let's read and understand the rest of v. 26.

Read the last two phrases: "The end of it shall be with a flood, and 'till the end of the war desolations are determined." Now this is a super-tricky passage. It's so tricky, in fact, that nobody wants to talk about it. No study Bibles, no commentaries, <u>nobody</u> would hardly touch this last sentence (with the exception of maybe one or two oblique references to it). I must confess that running into this problem (like we did a couple of pages ago) is starting to get a little bothersome! I'll grant you that this is a very difficult statement, but just because a passage is hard is not a good reason to shy away from it. For Pete's sake, at least *try* to figure it out, right? Well, that's what I intend to do here and now; I'm gonna give it the old college try.

First, let me show you what makes this such a tough nut to crack. Look at the sentences on either side. In the sentence just prior, which we already dissected, we saw that the Romans will destroy Jerusalem and the temple. I'm sure it's still fresh in your mind that this is what happened in A.D. 70, so this is a part of the prophecy that's been fulfilled. Now look at the first sentence of v. 27, which is on the other end of our sentence currently under the microscope. It reads: "Then he (the prince) shall confirm a covenant with many for one week..."

Notice that it starts out with the word "then," which breaks up the events of vs. 26 and 27 by an unspecified amount of time. This means that v. 27 begins with the seventieth week, which is the final section and seemingly the only unfulfilled portion of this prophecy. As a result, a casual reading of the last sentence of v. 26 seems to place this flood and "desolations" *before* the seventieth week and therefore make it the climax of the now-fulfilled 69 weeks. In fact, however, our sentence starts out with the words "The end of it..." This phrase (which likewise points to time or an epoch in time), at first reading, seems to be talking about the end of the destruction of Jerusalem and the temple.

What makes this sentence so hard to interpret is the fact that there is no known flood that took place during Rome's sacking of Jerusalem in A.D. 70. But notice the wording of the phrase right after the word "flood." We're told that "...'till the end of the war desolations are determined." I'm here to tell you that the war on Israel has never ended. Furthermore, the Roman conquest of Israel and the ensuing dispersion of the Jews resulted in the land of Canaan spending many centuries lying "desolate." Likewise this "flood," which is to come at "the end," hasn't happened yet.

Stay with me here. This last sentence of v. 26 is actually connected to the seventieth week, which is the focus of v. 27. (As a quick reminder, we still haven't answered the question of who the "prince" is. Don't forget that!) As we work toward the goal of unmasking the "prince," I want to see what we can learn from this "flood." Go to Revelation 12. The middle section of that chapter, vs. 7-12, talks about the war in heaven that ended with Michael and his angels tossing Satan off of heaven's porch and slamming the door in his face. Starting from there, we'll pick up the action in vs. 13-17.

Here we learn that Satan (called the "dragon" in this sequence), following his unsuccessful campaign against Michael, is confined to the earth. This puts him into a blinding rage. He pursues Israel, who is pictured here as the woman who gave birth to the male Child (i.e. the Messiah). However, Israel escapes into the wilderness for three and a half years, which infuriates the devil even more. The Scripture goes on to say that Satan will then attempt to murder the fleeing Jews with a flood, but the earth will open up and swallow the water before it can harm his beleaguered quarry. This will madden Satan greater still, and he will stomp off to fight the rest of God's elect.

Some commentaries suggest that this flood (as well as the flood of Daniel 9) is metaphorical, that it's a figure of speech for false teaching or something. But there's a hole in that theory. The Hebrew word "flood" in Dan. 9:26 and the Greek word for "flood" here both suggest a flood from a river. The Hebrew word refers to an "overflowing," as in a river overflowing its banks. The Greek word here in Revelation also points to that definition. The NASB even words it that way: "And the serpent poured water like a river out of his mouth after the woman, so that he might cause her to be swept away with the flood" (Rev. 12:15).

Consequently, I don't buy the argument that this flood is a symbol of anything else. Just read Rev. 12:16 again. There is no reason to spiritualize or allegorize or rationalize this flood. Satan is going to chase the children of Israel with a real flood of real water, but as we saw back in Chapter 20, it's going to take place at the midpoint of the Tribulation. There's no sense in trying to force this event into the pages of history, because it simply hasn't happened yet.

I know that reviewing this subject may seem a little excessive, especially since we touched on it earlier in the book. But because this is an area of Scripture that no one is willing to talk about much, I think it's important that we carefully and thoughtfully examine it. This is particularly true since I've found that it acts as something of a connecting rod between the events surrounding it and thus it helps us make more sense out of this entire prophecy.

With this in mind, go back to Dan. 9:26 and read the last sentence one more time. The end of the destruction of Jerusalem and the temple will be marked by a flood and "desolations." However, Jerusalem and the temple were already destroyed once before, and there was no flood. What gives? I'll tell you what gives: the Law of Double Fulfillment! Go on and read v. 27 now, which holds the key to both our "mystery prince" and this "flood" and "desolation." Just as v. 24 is the summary statement for the highlights of the 70-week prophecy, just as v. 25 is the signpost for when the Jews should be looking for their Messiah, and just as v. 26 gives us the short version of Messiah's death and a couple of hints about Antichrist, v. 27 accentuates the most important events of the Tribulation period (the "Seventieth Week").

Here's what I think has contributed to the confusion of so many scholars and commentators about the last sentence of v. 26. It seems, based solely on the few passing tiny remarks about it that I've come across, that they've understood the flood and desolations to be a part of the destruction of Jerusalem and the temple, which occurred in A.D. 70. (I'm sure that part of the reason for this is because v. 27 seems to be a natural starting point for the seventieth week. I'm going against the grain here by contending for the idea that the seventieth week actually starts here, in this last portion of v. 26.)

Remember what I said a little bit ago, that we're presently staring the Law of Double Fulfillment square in the face. I also said that I couldn't find a single book, article, commentary, or study Bible that was willing to directly take on this subject of the flood and desolations. As a result, I have no one to compare my thoughts to in regard to this, so I'm about to tell you things that you might not hear from anyone else. The chance exists, then, that I might have missed something important along the way, so be on your toes as we set to embark on a journey into the treacherous land of seldom discussed prophecy.

Chapter 42

The Abomination of Desolation

Before we launch into mostly uncultivated territories, I want to do a quick review. The Law of Double Fulfillment says what? Do you remember? It says that a prophetic event is fulfilled twice, once in part and then once in full. We know that the central figure in Dan. 9:26-27 has to be the Antichrist. He's the "prince to come" in v. 26, a man so important that we're told his nationality. This prince is going to sign a covenant with Israel that will start God's prophetic time clock one more time and finish out the yet-to-be-completed seventieth week. We see this in v. 27, where we also see that he will put an end to Israel's sacrificial system and he'll somehow make the city and/or temple vacant (or "desolate"). This is all rather confusing, I know, and I'm sorry to say that I'm about to make things worse. Be prepared to read this section two or three times in order for it to make sense. I know that's what I had to do!

All right, the Romans (or Europeans, in modern terminology) have destroyed Jerusalem and the temple (v. 26). Then this prince comes along and makes a treaty with "many" for one week (seven years), but he'll violate the terms of that treaty at the midpoint of this time period (v. 27). Just how will he violate this treaty? By bringing an end to sacrifice and offering. And where do the Jews make their sacrifices?

In the temple of Jerusalem! This is all review from what we learned way back in Chapter 3, so go back and read that section of the book again if you need to be refreshed. I'm returning now to the subject of the temple and the fact that it will be rebuilt, only to be defiled and completely destroyed at the midpoint of the Tribulation.

The most significant part of my argument here is that the temple will be rebuilt, and then it will be *completely* destroyed (Matt. 24:3). To strengthen my case for this twice-fulfilled prophecy, look at the fact that there are two mentions of destroying the temple in Dan. 9:26-27, and there are two time frames in which these events occur. In v. 26, the Romans will destroy Jerusalem and the temple at the end of the 69 weeks. Then, in v. 27, "the prince" will put an end to temple sacrifices. There is no unambiguous indication of the destruction of Jerusalem or of a *total* destruction of the temple in v. 27, but since Jesus explicitly predicted the latter, there must be an occasion where that happens. It's also important to keep in mind the fact that v. 27 tells us that it will be at the midpoint of the seventieth and final week when the sacrifices will abruptly end.

Now I've already spilled the beans a little bit when I said that the "prince" is the Antichrist. But how do I know that? Well, here's what we know about this prince from our text: (1) He's a Roman (i.e. European); and (2) He's the agent of peace for a treaty that involves Israel (we know this because he will violate the terms of that treaty by putting a stop to temple worship, so Israel <u>must</u> be the focus of the treaty). Now add to that the last half of v. 27, which reads: "And on the wing of abominations shall be one who makes desolate, even until the consummation, which is determined, is poured out on the desolate."

This is a very difficult sentence, so we'll need all the help we can get on this one. I'm going to start by examining a couple of other places in Daniel that also uses this same phraseology. The first place I want to take you is Chapter 11, which covers two distinct time periods of prophetic fulfillment. The first portion of this chapter (vs. 1-35) describes Persian and Grecian involvement in campaigns and transitions between East and West, between Asia and Europe. Verses 21-35 introduce us to a king of the North, a Syrian named Antiochus IV Epiphanes. He was an archetype of the coming final Antichrist, who is described in vs. 36-45. But I want to direct your attention back to one verse, v. 31, which predicts a heinous act of blasphemy by Antiochus: "And forces shall be mustered by him, and they shall defile the sanctuary fortress; then they shall take away the daily sacrifices, and place there the abomination of desolation."

Antiochus, whose title "Epiphanes" translates roughly to "manifest God," was called "Epimanes" (which means "madman") by the Jews whom he oppressed. For a summary of his treatment of the Jews, I want to quote from the apocryphal book of II Maccabees, 5:11-14; 6:1-11. Here's what it says about this madman, Antiochus:

> "And so, when these things were done, the king suspected that the Jews would desert

the alliance. And because of this, departing from Egypt with a raging soul, he indeed took the city by force. Moreover, he ordered the military to execute, and not to spare, anyone they met, and to ascend through the houses to slay. Therefore, a massacre occurred of youths and elders, an extermination of women and children, a killing of virgins and little ones. And so, over three whole days, eighty thousand were executed, forty thousand were imprisoned, and no small number were sold." (Now, 6:1-11): "But not much time later, the king sent a certain elder of Antioch, who compelled the Jews to transfer themselves from the laws of God and of their fathers, and also to contaminate the temple that was in Jerusalem, and to name it 'Jupiter of Olympus', and in Gerizim, 'Jupiter of Hospitality', exactly like those who inhabited the place. Yet the worst and most grievous thing of all was the onrush of evils. For the temple was full of the luxuries and carousings of the Gentiles, and of consorting with promiscuous women. And the women hurried themselves unreservedly into the sacred buildings, bringing in things that were not lawful. And even the altar was filled with illicit things, which were prohibited by the laws. And also the Sabbaths were not kept, and the solemn days of the fathers were not observed, neither did anyone simply confess himself to be a Jew. And so, they were led by bitter necessity, on the birthday of the king, to the sacrifices. And, when the holy things of Liber were celebrated, they were forced to go around crowned with the ivy of Liber. Then a decree went out to the neighboring cities of the Gentiles, suggested by the Ptolemeans, that they too should act in a similar manner against the Jews, to oblige them to sacrifice, and that those who were not willing to conform to the institutions of the Gentiles should be executed. Therefore, there was misery to be seen. For two women were denounced for having had their boys circumcised. These, with the infants suspended at their breasts, when they had publicly led them around the city, they cast down from the walls. Truly, others, meeting together in nearby caves and celebrating the Sabbath day secretly, when they had been discovered by Philip, were burned with fire, because they showed reverence to the observances of religion, deciding to help themselves by their own hand."[1]

That gives us a taste of what Antiochus was like. Dan. 11:31 says that he and his army would "defile the sanctuary," that they would "take away the daily sacrifices," and that "there" (i.e. the temple) they would place the "abomination of desolation." Hence, this verse helps us understand that the "abomination of desolation" is an act that is directly tied to the Jewish temple.

What exactly is this "abomination"? We can conclude that this abominable act, whatever it is, causes something to be made "desolate." It seems reasonable to assume, based on Dan. 11:31, that the place being made "desolate" will be the temple. From what we read in II Maccabees, we can certainly conclude that Antiochus' actions some 160 years before Jesus came were a foreshadowing (and partial fulfillment) of the prophecy of Dan. 9:27. In other words, Antiochus' actions were "abominable" enough that they defiled the temple to such a degree that it was no longer usable, thereby making it "desolate" (i.e. an uninhabited wasteland). Once the temple had been desecrated, it could no longer be used to make sacrifices that were acceptable to God.

Remember, it is theoretically possible for you to not need a Savior in order to get into heaven. All you have to do is live an absolutely perfect life and never commit one sin. But once you've sinned, just one little time, your chances of entering Heaven without Jesus are ZERO. That's another reason we know that Jesus was completely perfect. Had He ever committed just one sin, His sacrifice of Himself would have been rejected by the Father, which means that He would not have been raised from the dead and ascended into heaven. I bring this up here because Jesus referred to His own body as being the temple of God (cf. John 2:19-22). Jesus, the perfect, spotless Lamb of God, could only take away the sin of the world if He Himself were sinless. That's why the Jewish temple had to likewise remain spotless and ceremonially clean. To defile the temple would be to make its sacrifices useless.

Chapter 43

Time, Times, and Half a Time

Now remember that what we've seen up to this point, as far as Dan. 11:31 is concerned anyway, is only the first fulfillment of a twice-fulfilled prophecy. The question has to be asked: "How do we know that this prophecy is subject to the Law of Double Fulfillment?" That's actually an easily solved problem, as we have several exhibits to present that will make that case. First, we have seen more than one man whose traits align with portions of the description of "Antichrist" since the writing of Daniel, but no one has ever completely fit the bill. The Antichrist's ancestors destroyed Jerusalem and *mostly* destroyed the temple, but not entirely. Notice second that the <u>people destroyed</u> the temple in fulfillment of v. 26, while the Antichrist yet to come will unilaterally *defile* the temple in fulfillment of v. 27.

Third, and perhaps most significant of all (so far, anyway), we know for certain that no one has fulfilled the abomination prophecy of v. 27 because no one has signed a seven-year treaty with Israel yet. But wait, there's more! I said earlier that there are a "couple" (meaning two) more places in Daniel where the "abomination of desolation" is discussed. We looked at the first one, in Dan. 11:31. Now let's look at the other one, which is found in Dan. 12:11: "And from the time that the daily sacrifice is taken away, and the abomination of desolation is set up, there shall be one thousand two hundred and ninety days." This verse really seals the deal; there's NO WAY that this "abomination of desolation" has been fulfilled! There are two big reasons we know this, which I will address over the next couple of chapters.

To start with, there is a very important mention of a time period, namely the exact figure of 1,290 days. Just how long is 1,290 days? Answer: forty-three months (according to Jewish calendar reckoning), or three years and seven months. This is an interesting length of time, as it *almost* (but not exactly) matches up with the other prophetic scriptures that talk about "time, times, and half a time." I want to have you look at a couple of them briefly. Just back up a few verses and read Dan. 12:1-7. The archangel Michael, who is identified in v. 1 as a "prince" who has been assigned to protect the children of Israel, will be called into action. His calling will be in response to the "time of trouble" that will come upon the Jews, but he will be instrumental in saving them.

We see in v. 2 a description of a resurrection of the dead. You might recognize this as the point of contention where some prophecy scholars say that this is when the righteous OT saints are raised to life at the end of the Tribulation. I, on the other hand, believe it is a reference to the Rapture for the righteous dead, and for the wicked it will be the Second Resurrection where they will be sentenced to everlasting perdition (cf. Rev. 20:5-6). In short, these are two resurrections that take place at two different times. There is the First Resurrection for the righteous (the Rapture, which will put a period on the Age of Grace), and then there's the Second Resurrection for the lost at the end of the Millennium (cf. John 5:28-29).

The first three verses, then, give us an overview of the Tribulation and the judgment of all humanity. Then, in v. 4, Daniel is instructed to seal up — or hide the meaning of — the words of this prophecy until the last days. This passage ends with Daniel being given a vision of two more angels and a man wearing a linen garment, who is most likely the Lord Jesus in preincarnate form. Daniel asks these heavenly beings how long it will be before the fulfillment of the things of which he was told, and the Lord replied that it would be for "a time, times, and half a time."

We've seen this language before, in places like Dan. 7:25; Rev. 12:14. Notice in Revelation that Israel (the "woman") runs into the wilderness, and if you recall that Israel was chased by that flood we studied a short ways back (Rev. 12:15-16), we can conclude that this must be the Great Tribulation, the last "time, times, and half a time" we see in v. 14. In fact, we're told that the exact length of time meant by that phrase is 42 months; just back up a little and read v. 6: "Then the woman fled into the wilderness, where she has a place prepared by God, that they should feed her there one thousand two hundred and sixty days."

Hence, forty-two months and 1,260 days and "time, times, and half a time" are all the same thing. Staying here in Revelation, we see that there are a couple more significant uses of this time period. Just back up a chapter and read 11:1-3. The chapter begins with an angel, who gives John a measuring rod and commands him to take measurements of the temple. The angel then tells his guest that the outer court of the temple is not to be measured, because it will be occupied by the Gentiles for a period of forty-two months. The angel follows this comment with v. 3, which is the first reference to the two witnesses.

I have already explained that the one thing I'm waiting to hear, more than anything else in the world, is for the Jewish people to start hollering that they want their temple back. Remember, the Old Testament message of salvation was pictured through the daily sacrifices at the temple. The New Covenant was wrought by our Lord Jesus through the once-for-all sacrifice at the cross of Calvary. Those are two very different and conflicting messages, so the Church (God's current temple here on earth) won't be here once the Jewish temple is back up and running.

I'm not trying to say that the Jews, through their temple sacrifices, will be providing a valid means of salvation, so don't misconstrue my point. What I'm saying here is that the Church Age is rightly called the Age of Grace, and that the Rapture will bring about the end of this age. The Tribulation is primarily for the Jews, and as such their temple will be the message of salvation they'll be preaching, wrong though it shall be. They are already back in their land, they are their own sovereign nation once again, and they are striving to be the unique culture that they once were. The only thing missing from Israel's repertoire now is their religion, and one day soon that missing piece will be put in place. If you think the world hates the Jews now, just you wait until they're worshiping God after the Old Testament pattern! (By the way, I didn't forget about the difference in time between the 1,290 days versus the 1,260 days. I will address that issue in a little more detail in Chapter 46.)

Chapter 44

The Two Witnesses

Keeping our place in Rev. 11:1-3, this temple (mentioned in vs. 1-2a) is going to be the rebuilt temple of the Tribulation. (Keep this Tribulation Temple in mind for the remainder of our time together. We'll be coming back to it again before long.) But back to our text, v. 2b says that the Gentiles will have control of Jerusalem (the "holy city") for forty-two months. We know that this 3-1/2 year period is the Great Tribulation, the last half of the Tribulation. How do we know that? Because of what we saw in the previous chapter when we looked at Rev. 12:6, 14. The Jews will occupy Jerusalem during the first half of the Tribulation, i.e. the first forty-two months (or the first 1,260 days, or the first "time, times, and half a time"). Afterward, Antichrist is going to run them off into the wilderness somewhere, and God will supernaturally protect and care for them for the last 3-1/2 years.

To review, Satan runs the children of Israel out of Jerusalem, and Antichrist and "the Gentiles" come in and take over. It will be during this time (still at the halfway point of the Tribulation) that another monumental event will take place, that being the killing and raising of the two witnesses. Go back to Chapter 11 again, and this time read vs. 3-6. In these verses, the angel illumines John about two unnamed men who will serve as witnesses to the whole world (we very briefly touched on this in the previous chapter). They will be given a ministry that's going to last exactly 42 months, during which time they'll be utterly indestructible. They will kill any person who tries to hurt them by burning him up with the supernatural fiery breath of their mouths, and they will prevent rain from falling upon the earth throughout the entirety of their time here. But that's not all. They will turn the waters into blood, and they will send plagues upon the earth whenever they desire.

Back in Chapter 16, I made the case for my belief that these two men are none other than Moses and Elijah. However, we're not going to plow that ground again, because what I want to focus on this time is the 1,260 days (the time period we're given in Rev. 11:3). It is worth noting that the two witnesses have a highly specialized ministry. Notice also here in v. 3 that these two men are wearing sackcloth. Keep your finger here and go back and read Isa. 20:2; Dan. 9:3. Sackcloth robes are the apparel of choice for God's prophets to the people of Israel. Also, remember that theirs is a message of judgment, which is in keeping with the principle of Deut. 17:6; 19:15.

Okay, let's return to Revelation 11. We have two witnesses, wearing the attire of Jewish prophets, and testifying in Jerusalem for 3-1/2 years. Now look at v. 4. Here, God calls them "olive trees" and "lampstands." This is a very important designation being given to these two men. This simple moniker gives us deep insight into the men's message as well as their identities. While it doesn't necessarily help us *name* the two prophets, it helps us tremendously in terms of our understanding what kind of men they are.

Turn back to your Old Testament again and find Zechariah 4; while you're looking for it, call to your memory what we know about these witnesses. Remember that there are two of them, which means that they're proclaiming judgment. Remember also that they're stationed in Jerusalem (we see that in Rev. 11:7-8; their dead bodies, after they've been murdered by Antichrist, will lie uncovered in the streets of Jerusalem). And third, remember that their clothing, which is sackcloth, is that of Jewish prophets. At this point, there's no way to get out of the conclusion that these two men are Jews, and they're preaching to a Jewish audience.

When you get to Zechariah 4, read vs. 1-3. Zechariah is given a vision of a lampstand and two olive trees. This should certainly get our attention, shouldn't it? All right, keep going. Read vs. 4-10: "So I answered and spoke to the angel who talked with me, saying, 'What are these, my lord?' Then the angel who talked with me answered and said to me, 'Do you not know what these are?' And I said, 'No, my lord.' So he answered and said to me: 'This is the word of the Lord to Zerubbabel: 'Not by might nor by power, but by My Spirit,' Says the Lord of hosts. 'Who are you, O great mountain? Before Zerubbabel you shall become a plain! And he shall bring forth the capstone With shouts of 'Grace, grace to it!'" Moreover the word of the Lord came to me, saying: 'The hands of Zerubbabel Have laid the foundation of this temple; His hands shall also finish it. Then you will know That the Lord of hosts has sent Me to you. For who has despised the day of small things? For these seven rejoice to see The plumb line in the hand of Zerubbabel. They are the eyes of the Lord, Which scan to and fro throughout the whole earth.'"

Without getting too terribly deep into this passage, let's look at a couple of important highlights. First, the prophet is given a message specifically for Zerubbabel. The message boils down to v. 9, where it is said that Zerubbabel will successfully rebuild the temple, which was intended to be a word of encouragement to all Israel.

The other part that's important for us to glean is found in vs. 11-14: "Then I answered and said to him, 'What are these two olive trees – at the right of the lampstand and at its left?' And I further answered and said to him, 'What are these two olive branches that drip into the receptacles of the two gold pipes from which the golden oil drains?' Then he answered me and said, "Do you not know what these are?' And I said, 'No, my lord.' So he said, "These are the two anointed ones, who stand beside the Lord of the whole earth.'" The message of the rebuilding of the temple and the testimony that the message is true comes from where? Verses 11-12 – the olive trees and the lampstand! Does this not give us tremendous help?

Now go back to Revelation 11. We have two Jewish men wearing the sackcloth of Jewish prophets standing in Jerusalem and preaching to a Jewish audience. Evidently, they'll be preaching judgment (v. 5 says that they'll kill people that want to harm them, so their message is obviously not very popular with some people, and v. 6 says they'll bring plagues down on the earth just like those that Moses did on Egypt). The really big message they'll be preaching, though, according to what we just saw in Zechariah, is the rebuilding of the temple!

This brings us full circle to the observation that I made a little bit ago, that the ministry of these two witnesses must be in the first half of the Tribulation. Based on everything we've seen, it's certain that these Jewish men in a Jewish city wearing Jewish garments giving a Jewish message to *Gentiles* would make absolutely no sense! Since the Jews haven't been run off by Antichrist, they're still in Jerusalem. Since Antichrist and the Gentiles will have control of Jerusalem for the last 3-1/2 years, and since the Tribulation will last for seven years, and since the two witnesses will minister for 3-1/2 years to the Jews in Jerusalem, we're left with but one logical conclusion: this ministry of the two witnesses can *only* be in the first 1,260 days (or 3-1/2 years) of the Tribulation!

Finally, let's look at how the ministry of these two mighty men comes to an end. We're given that information in Rev. 11:7-13: "When they finish their testimony, the beast that ascends out of the bottomless pit will make war against them, overcome them, and kill them. And their dead bodies will lie in the street of the great city which spiritually is called Sodom and Egypt, where also our Lord was crucified. Then those from the peoples, tribes, tongues, and nations will see their dead bodies three-and-a-half days, and not allow their dead bodies to be put into graves. And those who dwell on the earth will rejoice over them, make merry, and send gifts to one another, because these two prophets tormented those who dwell on the earth. Now after the three-and-a-half days the breath of life from God entered them, and they stood on their feet, and great fear fell on those who saw them. And they heard a loud voice from heaven saying to them, 'Come up here.' And they ascended to heaven in a cloud, and their enemies saw them. In the same hour there was a great earthquake, and a tenth of the city fell. In the earthquake seven thousand people were killed, and the rest were afraid and gave glory to the God of heaven."

In v. 7, Antichrist finally kills them. This is right at the midpoint of the Tribulation, right when the Tribulation will become the Great Tribulation. The remaining verses we just read tell us about the witnesses being raised back to life after 3-1/2 days, the world rejoicing over their deaths, and their ascension into heaven while the world looks on and panics with great fear. But that leaves us with one really important subject: the temple!

Chapter 45

The Tribulation Temple

Go back to Dan. 9:27 and look at the part that reads: "Then he (Antichrist) shall confirm a covenant with many for one week, but in the middle of the week he shall bring an end to sacrifice and offering." Where do sacrifices and offerings take place? The temple! If Antichrist is going to bring an end to sacrifice and offering, that *must* mean that sacrifices and offerings are taking place. That, in turn, must also necessarily mean that the temple, during the Tribulation, must be in existence AND in operation! That's why I'm keeping my ear to the ground, listening for the sound of hammer and saw in Jerusalem, the sound of a Jewish temple being built! If we haven't been sucked out of this world in Rapture by the time the Jews start screaming for their temple, it won't be very long after that until we are!

You see, Antichrist will be coming into Jerusalem at the midpoint of the Tribulation, and he's going to do several things. He's going to kill the two witnesses, he's going to run the Jews out of Jerusalem, he himself will appear to have been killed and then subsequently "resurrected," and he's going to destroy the temple. Now let's spend a little more time on this temple. First, let's settle this unresolved problem of the Law of Double Fulfillment. Think back to Dan. 9:26, where we saw that the people of the prince to come destroyed Jerusalem and most of the temple in A.D. 70. When

Antichrist comes on the scene, he is going to sign a seven-year treaty with Israel (we see that in v. 27); the signing of that treaty will start God's prophetic clock once more. This is the exact moment when the seventieth and final week of Daniel's prophecy begins.

Remember also that the prophecy of v. 26 regarding the temple is simply its destruction. But the prediction of v. 27 is Antichrist destroying the temple in a specific manner, that being the "abomination of desolation." The amillennialists and the preterists all say that this occurred when Antiochus came in and did what he did long about 167 B.C. To their credit, those in the "non-futurist" camp of whatever stripe are certainly correct when they say that Antiochus' actions fit the bill of this destruction and defilement of the temple.

However, there are two major prophecies regarding the temple that remain unfulfilled, and the opponents of premillennialism have no answer for them. First, go back and reread Matt. 24:1-2. As we've discussed several times, the complete destruction of the temple has not happened yet; there's still the matter of that Wailing Wall. But there's also another prophecy regarding the temple that hasn't been fulfilled. Coming once again from the lips of our Lord, and also here in this very same chapter, read vs. 15-16: "'Therefore when you see the 'abomination of desolation,' spoken of by Daniel the prophet, standing in the holy place' (whoever reads, let him understand), 'then let those who are in Judea flee to the mountains.'"

As if it weren't enough that Jesus said that every single stone of the temple would be thrown down, He goes on to tell us in this same sermon that there is still a day coming when there will be <u>another</u> "abomination of desolation." There was no abominable act against the temple, no defilement of it, in A.D. 70. It was merely *mostly* destroyed by the Romans. But hold on, there's still more! Notice in v. 15 that Jesus' words were for people who would *read* the book of Matthew, which would not have been possible until *after* this disciple's gospel account was written and the New Testament was completed! Therefore, the only feasible interpretation of this passage is that it is referring to events that can only take place at some point after the closing of the canon of Scripture, which was in ca. A.D. 95.

Think back to what we were talking about in regard to the two witnesses in Revelation 11. You will recall that one of their primary messages (maybe even <u>the</u> primary message) will be in regard to the temple, its being rebuilt, and its function. We've already seen that the temple will be in operation during the first half of the Tribulation. In fact, it may be a safe bet that those two witnesses are to be stationed on the temple grounds! So how do we make sense of the prophetic message from these bizarre preachers? How is it that the witnesses will be proclaiming a coming temple while they're standing in front of an already-existing temple? The answer to that is much easier than you might think, and we even touched on that answer only a few chapters ago.

Our elucidation comes from John's gospel: "So the Jews answered and said to Him, 'What sign do You show to us, since You do these things?' Jesus answered and said to them, 'Destroy this temple, and in three days I will raise it up.' Then the Jews said, 'It has taken forty-six years to build this temple, and will You raise it up in three days?' But He was speaking of the temple of His body. Therefore, when He had risen from the dead, His disciples remembered that He had said this to them; and they believed the Scripture and the word which Jesus had said" (John 2:18-22).

JESUS is the Temple; JESUS is the coming place of worship, NOT the structure standing behind those two prophets. They know that the blood of bulls and goats don't take away sin. They know that this temple is no longer necessary. These two witnesses are going to infuriate just about everyone! They'll anger the Gentiles, who hate Jesus anyway, and they'll incense the Jews, who are trying to please God in an outmoded manner. *Everybody* is gonna want to kill those two witnesses! The witnesses' message to the Gentiles will be: "Repent, for the kingdom of Heaven is at hand!" And their message to the Jews will be: "Stop your worthless sacrifices at this useless temple. The real Temple, whom you crucified, is on His way!"

Antichrist is going to come in and take over the temple, defile it, and ultimately he'll completely destroy it (i.e. he'll throw down every last stone)! What will that look like? II Thess. 2:1-4: "Now, brethren, concerning the coming of our Lord Jesus Christ and our gathering together to Him, we ask you, not to be soon shaken in mind or troubled, either by spirit or by word or by letter, as if from us, as though the day of Christ had come. Let no one deceive you by any means; for that Day will not come unless the falling away comes first, and the man of sin is revealed, the son of perdition, who opposes and exalts himself above all that is called God or that is worshiped, so that he sits as God in the temple of God, showing himself that he is God."

The Day of the Lord is coming in conjunction with the coming of Antichrist, and he's going to go into the temple and set himself up as being God. How's that for blasphemy and a defilement of the temple? How's that for an "abomination of desolation"? When these things happen, when the Son of Perdition demands to be worshiped at the temple, the children of Israel will flee Jerusalem and run into "the wilderness" (wherever that will be), and thus will begin the Great Tribulation.

Chapter 46

Christ's Victory and Antichrist's Doom

A little more precision regarding Antichrist's blasphemous acts are found in Rev. 13:1-8: "Then I stood on the sand of the sea. And I saw a beast rising up out of the sea, having seven heads and ten horns, and on his horns ten crowns, and on his heads a blasphemous name. Now the beast which I saw was like a leopard, his feet were like the feet of a bear, and his mouth like the mouth of a lion. The dragon gave him his power, his throne, and great authority. And I saw one of his heads as if it had been mortally wounded, and his deadly wound was healed. And all the world marveled and followed the beast. So they worshiped the dragon who gave authority to the beast; and they worshiped the beast, saying, 'Who is like the beast? Who is able to make war with him?' And he was given a mouth speaking great things and blasphemies, and he was given authority to continue for forty-two months. Then he opened his mouth in blasphemy against God, to blaspheme His name, His tabernacle, and those who dwell in heaven. It was granted to him to make war with the saints and to overcome them. And authority was given him over every tribe, tongue, and nation. All who dwell on the earth will worship him, whose names have not been written in the Book of Life of the Lamb slain from the foundation of the world."

According to v. 3, Antichrist will appear to have been killed and resurrected, so he'll be worshiped by the entire unbelieving world (vs. 4, 8). Verse 5 says that he'll be given total control over the whole world for – there it is again – forty-two months. Finally, vs. 6-7 say that he will utter great and blasphemous things, and he will blaspheme God and His "tabernacle" (which possibly is a reference to the temple, Jesus, or both), and he'll make war with the Christians, the new converts won during the Tribulation. Evidently, it will also be during this time that Antichrist will <u>completely</u> destroy the temple.

For one last look at what Antichrist will be doing during this brief period, let's go back to Daniel and read 11:36: "Then the king shall do according to his own will: he shall exalt and magnify himself above every god, shall speak blasphemies against the God of gods, and shall prosper till the wrath has been accomplished; for what has been determined shall be done." Notice that, according to the last two phrases of that verse, Antichrist is on a tight schedule that has been determined, not by him, but by God. And how long will that time period be? Forty-two months.

This leaves us with only a couple of unanswered questions. First, let's go back and look at the 1,290 days mentioned in Dan. 12:11. We've established already that 3-1/2 years, time and times and half a time, forty-two months, and 1,260 days all refer to the same amount of time. But what's with this extra thirty days? How does this fit? To be candid, I can't say with any real degree of certainty, but I do see two viable possibilities. One is given by John MacArthur in his study Bible. He writes: "From the intrusion of the abomination, there follow 1,290 days, including 1,260 which make up the last 3-1/2 years of the final 7 years, then 30 days more, possibly to allow for the judgment of the living subsequent to Christ's return (cf. Mt. 24:29-31; 25:31-46), before millennial kingdom blessings begin."[1]

That's one possible explanation, the idea that there is an extra thirty days of this prophecy that spill over into the Second Coming and commencement of the 1,000-year reign of Jesus. But I also want to throw out a second possibility. Maybe the abomination of desolation will be set up thirty days *before* the exact midpoint of the Tribulation, so the abomination/destruction will be 1,290 days from the end of the Tribulation, the Battle of Armageddon, and the Parousia.

By the way, do we know exactly what the abomination of desolation will be, beyond the blasphemous words of Antichrist and him setting himself up as God in the temple? Not in so many words, perhaps, but we are given a big clue. Go back to Revelation again and read about the ministry of the False Prophet: "Then I saw another beast coming up out of the earth, and he had two horns like a lamb and spoke like a dragon. And he exercises all the authority of the first beast in his presence, and causes the earth and those who dwell in it to worship the first beast, whose deadly wound was healed. He performs great signs, so that he even makes fire come down from heaven on the earth in the sight of men. And he deceives those who dwell on the earth by those signs which he was granted to do in the sight of the beast, telling those who dwell on the earth to make an image to the beast who was wounded by the sword and lived. He was granted power to give breath to the image of the beast, that the image of the beast should both speak and cause as many as would not worship the image of the beast to be killed" (Rev. 13:11-15).

There will be some sort of statue of Antichrist that will be erected under the supervision of the False Prophet. Under penalty of death, the False Prophet will see to it that *everyone* worships the statue. So you have Antichrist, sitting in the temple and demanding worship as God, and you have Antichrist's statue, probably either in or very near the temple, that everyone must likewise worship. Here we have a violation of the first two commandments: putting someone other than God above God, and worship of a graven image (aka idolatry). That makes a pretty good recipe for an "abomination of desolation," doesn't it?

Well, with that, we're roundin' third and headin' home. We've only got two phrases left to look at, and they won't take long. Go back to Daniel 9, and read the very last phrase of v. 26: "And 'till the end of the war desolations are determined." What does that mean? I think that the "war" here is THE war, the war started by Satan against Adam and Eve in the Garden. It's the war over truth, the war over the souls of men. (By extension, that war has always raged against Israel and, now, the church. The devil hates all of God's people!)

When will this war end? At the very end of time, at the end of the Millennium. One last battle, one last confrontation between God and Satan: "Now when the thousand years have expired, Satan will be released from his prison and will go out to deceive the nations which are in the four corners of the earth, Gog and Magog, to gather them together to battle, whose number is as the sand of the sea. They went up on the breadth of the earth and surrounded the camp of the saints and the beloved city. And fire came down from God out of heaven and devoured them. The devil, who deceived them, was cast into the lake of fire and brimstone where the beast and the false prophet are. And they will be tormented day and night forever and ever" (Rev. 20:7-10). All this phrase means is that "desolations" (or "rebellion against God in one form or another") are predetermined by God and kept under His close supervision at all times. They are subject to God's absolute control, and they will not completely go away until the very end of the war between God and Satan, at the very end of time and all of history.

Now v. 27 has been almost completely opened to us. The verse opens with a mention of a seven-year "covenant," or treaty that involves "many." Who exactly are the many? It certainly includes Israel, because the very next phrase says that "...in the middle of the week (i.e. the midpoint of the Tribulation) he shall bring an end to sacrifice and offering." (You may recall that we discussed this at length a while back.) If Antichrist is going to *violate* a treaty that involves

Israel, then it's only logical that he must have previously *signed* a treaty that involves Israel. We've seen, at least in generalities, how Antichrist will accomplish the abomination of desolation, put an end to the temple's operations, and will ultimately throw every last stone of the temple complex to the ground.

The only thing left for us to learn now is the very last phrase of v. 27: "...Even until the consummation, which is determined, is poured out on the desolate." The NASB actually words this better, as it more accurately states: "...even until a complete destruction, one that is decreed, is poured out on the one who makes desolate." That rendering makes a lot more sense, and I think all that's necessary here is that we take these words at face value. The "complete destruction," which has been predetermined or "decreed," seems to refer to the entire seven-year Tribulation period. Then there's the "complete destruction" of the one who made the "desolation." That's easily enough understood, isn't it? That would be the Antichrist! And Antichrist, the "desolator," will himself be completely destroyed by the Lord at the very end of the Tribulation period, at the very end of exactly seven years, at the very end of the seventieth week of Daniel's prophecy.

How will the two beasts' fifteen minutes of fame play out? Scripture tells us: "Now I saw heaven opened, and behold, a white horse. And He who sat on him was called Faithful and True, and in righteousness He judges and makes war. His eyes were like a flame of fire, and on His head were many crowns. He had a name written that no one knew except Himself. He was clothed with a robe dipped in blood, and His name is called The Word of God. And the armies in heaven, clothed in fine linen, white and clean, followed Him on white horses. Now out of His mouth goes a sharp sword, that with it He should strike the nations. And He Himself will rule them with a rod of iron. He Himself treads the winepress of the fierceness and wrath of Almighty God. And He has on His robe and on His thigh a name written: 'KING OF KINGS AND LORD OF LORDS.' Then I saw an angel standing in the sun; and he cried with a loud voice, saying to all the birds that fly in the midst of heaven, 'Come and gather together for the supper of the great God, that you may eat the flesh of kings, the flesh of captains, the flesh of mighty men, the flesh of horses and of those who sit on them, and the flesh of all people, free and slave, both small and great.' And I saw the beast, the kings of the earth, and their armies, gathered together to make war against Him who sat on the horse and against His army. The beast was captured, and with him the false prophet who worked signs in his presence, by which he deceived those who received the mark of the beast and those who worshiped his image. These two were cast alive into the lake of fire burning with brimstone. And the rest were killed with the sword which proceeded from the mouth of Him who sat on the horse. And all the birds were filled with their flesh" (Rev. 19:11-21).

We Christians in this Age of Grace will be raptured and taken into heaven before any of this prophecy comes to pass, as we are not "appointed to wrath" (Rom. 5:9; I Thess. 1:10; 5:9-10). However, we'll have a front row seat for the destruction of the two beasts (Antichrist and the False Prophet), when we come with the King of all kings and the Lord of all lords. When that time comes, there will only be one thing left for you to do: **CHOOSE YOUR HORSE!!**

THE END

Epilogue

You may have noticed that conspicuously absent from this book was any mention of the United States in regard to end-time prophecy. I have been asked many times if I see our beloved nation anywhere in Bible prophecy. When I tell them no, the inevitable follow-up question is, "Why not?" My stock reply is that I don't see America in Bible prophecy because America is not anywhere in the Bible. God loves America, and He loves Americans. But the greatest and most important nation in the world is not and never will be the USA. God loves and cherishes Israel above all people and all nations. They are the apple of God's eye (Zech. 2:6-8). God has always had it in His mind to make Israel His special possession, His "chosen people." This unique plan was launched by the Lord in Genesis 12 with the call of Abraham, and He has never once deviated from it. Just when you think the days look the very darkest for that tiny dot on the map – and they are in for some exceedingly rough times ahead – God will rescue them and protect them in ways that will stagger the imagination.

As I write this, I am about to finish reading the Bible all the way through for the eleventh time in the past twelve years. I have made it a discipline to read the Bible from Genesis through Revelation every year, and I read it in a different translation each year. I want to recommend this practice to you. Whether you change translations from one year to the next is a matter of personal taste, but if you have never read the entire

Bible before, there's no time like the present to start a new habit. I will warn you that once you've read it through for the first time, you'll probably be asking yourself things like, "What in the world did that book say?"

However, something miraculous takes place between the first and second years. The instant you start over and begin your second tour, things start to gel in your mind and the primary themes of Scripture begin to make a whole lot more sense. As you read for the second and third and fourth times, entire doctrines bubble up and rise to the surface. One such doctrine – and it's a biggie – is that it is extremely clear that God has exalted the little nation of Israel to a place of preeminence over all the other nations of the world. A Jew cannot bypass the cross and enter into God's kingdom any more easily than a Gentile can. However, there's a day coming when all Israel shall be saved (Rom. 11:26-27).

If you have read this entire book, you and I have become connected. You have experienced what is on my heart, and I pray that it resonates with yours. But I realize that I am a fallen man with limited understanding, and there are things I have shared with you here that may not be perfectly in line with God's unfolding plan. That's why I urge you to read the Bible for yourself and to acquire a thirst for all of God's wisdom made available to you through it. There are no shortcuts. As much as I appreciate you reading my book, it is my prayer that you search the Scriptures every day and compare *all* things with the precious Word of God (Acts 17:11).

One last thing before I go. While I may not have everything nailed down perfectly, there are some things discussed in these pages that I do not doubt, not even a little bit. One such topic is that of the Rapture. Not only am I 100% confident that Jesus will come and carry every last one of His followers, both the quick and the dead, back to the Father's house, I'm also equally certain that it will happen *before* one second of the Tribulation clock has ticked off. If you happen to have read this book after there has been a mysterious disappearance of many thousands of people from every corner of the globe, I plead with you to refuse to believe the lies that the world's governments and media personalities will tell you. The one thing they'll never say is the one thing that will have happened; we'll have gone home to be with our Lord. If this is the case, you are in the period the Bible calls the Tribulation. It's too late for you to miss the judgment of God, which will last for exactly seven years. But if you haven't taken Jesus as your Lord and Master, and if there has been any talk of a seven-year treaty that somehow involves the nation of Israel, please do that right now.

Rough times lie ahead for you, but there is nothing that can happen in this world that will even come close to how bad it will be in eternity without Christ. I beg you, dear friend. Ask God to forgive your sins and to send His Son Jesus into your heart and life and for Him to be your Savior and Lord, and do it right now. If you allow Jesus to take all of your sins, He will give you all of His perfect righteousness in their place.

Even so, come, Lord Jesus!

Appendix A

Preterist

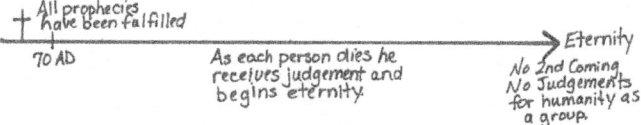

Amillennialist

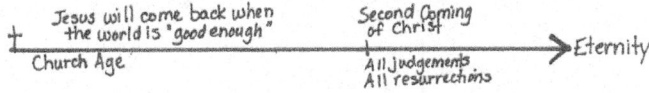

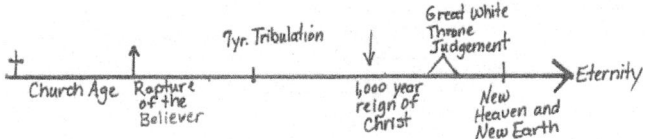

Appendix B

Timeline of Revelation

	New Heaven and Earth (Ch. 21-22)
	The Judgments (20:11-15)
	Satan Thrown into the Lake of Fire (20:10)
	Satan Released to Deceive the Nations (20:7-9)
	The Millennial Kingdom (20:4-6)
	Satan Bound for 1,000 Years (20:1-3)
	Antichrist and False Prophet Thrown into Lake of Fire (19:20)
	Second Coming of Christ (19:11-19)
	Battle of Armageddon (19:11-19)
	Destruction of Commercial Babylon (Ch. 18)
7th Bowl	Massive Earthquake (16:18-19)
6th Bowl	Euphrates Dried Up (16:12-14)
5th Bowl	Darkness and Pain (16:10-11)
4th Bowl	Sun Scorches the Earth (16:8-9)
3rd Bowl	Fresh Water Turned into Blood (16:4)
2nd Bowl	Sea Turned into Blood (16:3)
1st Bowl	Boils (sores) (16:2)
	Destruction of Religious Babylon (17:3-18)
	False Prophet Forces Worship of Antichrist (13:11-18)
	Israel Flees Antichrist (12:6, 13-17)
	Antichrist Stages his death and resurrection (13:3,12,14)
	Satan Kicked Out of Heaven (12:7-12)
7th Trumpet	Earthquake and Huge Hail (11:15-19)
6th Trumpet	200 Million Angelic Warriors (9:13-21)
5th Trumpet	Demonic Locusts (9:1-12)
4th Trumpet	Skies Darkened (8:12-13)
3rd Trumpet	Fresh Water Poisoned (8:10-11)
2nd Trumpet	Sea Turned to Blood (8:8-9)
1st Trumpet	Killing Vegetation (8:7)
7th Seal	Prelude to Trumpet Judgments (8:1-6)
	Harvest of Those Saved by the 144,000 (7:9-17)
Interlude	The 144,000 sealed (7:1-8)
6th Seal	Upheaval in the Heavens (6:12-17)
5th Seal	Martyrdom (6:9-11)
4th Seal	Death (6:7-8)
3rd Seal	Famine (6:5-6)
2nd Seal	War (6:3-4)
	Two Witnesses Preach for 3-1/2 years (11:1-14)
	World Divided into 10 Kingdoms (17:12-17)
1st Seal of Tribulation	Revealing of Antichrist (6:1-2)
	Our Worship in Heaven (4:3-5:14)
	Rapture (4:1-2)
	Church Age (Ch. 2-3)
	Intro. to Risen Lord (1:9-18)

Bibliography

Unless otherwise indicated, Scripture quotations are taken from the THE NEW KING JAMES VERSION. Copyright 1982 by Thomas Nelson, Inc. Used by permission. All rights reserved.

Chapter 2: How Do We Know We're in the Last Days?

1. "The Speed of Information," *The Technium,* 2006. This information taken from Wallace Henley, *Globequake: Living in the Unshakeable Kingdom While the World Falls Apart* (Nashville: Thomas Nelson, 2012), Ch. 1, note #13.

2. "Maastricht Treaty," *Wikipedia,* accessed September 2014, http://www.en.wikipedia.org/wiki/Maastricht_Treaty.

Chapter 4: Two More Signs

1. "Nuns on the Bus," *Wikipedia,* accessed September 2014, http://www.en.wikipedia.org/wiki/Nuns_on_the_Bus.

2. "Pope Benedict to Become First Pontiff in 600 Years to Resign," *Fox News,* February 11, 2013. Article online at http://www.foxnews.com/world/2013/02/11/pope-benedict-xvi-to-resign-at-end-february/.

3. "Pope Francis Discusses Gay Catholics: 'Who Am I to Judge?'", *The Two-Way (Breaking News From NPR)*, July 29, 2013. Article online at http://www.npr.org/blogs/thetwo-way/2013/07/29/206622682/pope-francis-discusses-gay-catholics-who-am-i-to-judge.

4. "Pope Francis Says Atheists Can Do Good and Go to Heaven Too!", *Catholic Online*, May 30, 2013. Article online at http://www.catholic.org/news/hf/faith/story.php?id=51077.

Chapter 11: Why Will There Be a Tribulation?

1. John MacArthur, *The MacArthur Study Bible (NKJV)* (Nashville, Word Publishing, 1997), pg. 32.

Chapter 14: Worship Before the Throne

1. John MacArthur, *The MacArthur Study Bible (NKJV)* (Nashville, Word Publishing, 1997), pg. 1998.

2. Ibid, pg. 1249.

3. Ibid, pgs. 1753-54.

4. J. Vernon McGee, *Thru the Bible with J. Vernon McGee, Vol. 5* (Nashville, Thomas Nelson Publishers, 1983), pg. 253.

5. Ibid, pg. 254.

Chapter 17: Hell Pays a Visit

1. "U.S. and World Population Clock," *U.S. Census Bureau,* accessed December 2013, http://www.census.gov/popclock/

2. "Global Christianity – A Report on the Size and Distribution of the World's Christian Population," *Pew Research,* accessed December 2013, http://www.pewforum.org/2011/12/19/global-christianity-exec/

3. "In U.S., 77% Identify as Christian," *Gallup.com* website, accessed December 2013, http://www.gallup.com/poll/159548/identify-christian.aspx

4. "U.S. and World Population Clock," *U.S. Census Bureau,* accessed December 2013, http://www.census.gov/popclock/

Chapter 18: The 144,000

1. "Facts About Jehovah's Witnesses", *JWFacts.com,* accessed September 2014, http://www.jwfacts.com/watchtower/144000.php.

2. "Just 144,000? Really?", *Adventist Review,* accessed September 2014, http://archives.adventistreview.org/article/2914/archives/issue-2009-1530/just-144-000-really. This article cites *The Advent Review and Sabbath Herald,* Mar. 9, 1905, which quotes *The SDA Bible Commentary,* vol. 7, pg. 970. The quote, which is from the writings of Ellen G. White, reads: "Let us strive with all the power that God has given us to be among the hundred and forty-four thousand."

Chapter 19: The Trumpet Judgments

1. "Chernobyl Disaster", *Wikipedia*, accessed September 2014, http://en.m.wikipedia.org/wiki/Chernobyl_disaster . Also see "Chernobyl Accident 1986," *World Nuclear Association*, accessed September 2014, http://www.world-nuclear.org/info/Safety-and-Security/Safety-of-Plants/Chernobyl-Accident/.

2. "Thomas Robert Malthus", *Wikipedia*, accessed September 2014, http://en.m.wikipedia.org/wiki/Thomas_Robert_Malthus.

Chapter 21: The Seven Bowls

1. "Volleyball from the Sky," *NOAA*, accessed July 2014, http://www.noaa.gov/features/02_monitoring/hailstone.html

Chapter 29: The Second Death

1. David Jeremiah, *The Jeremiah Study Bible (NKJV)* (Worthy Publishing), pg. 1866.

Chapter 30: Global Warming

1. Ted Merritt, *More Than Intelligence*, an unpublished essay written ca. 2009.

Chapter 32: The New Jerusalem

1. "How Many Babies Are Born Every Day in the World?", *Answers.com*, accessed August 2014,

http://www.answers.com/Q/How_many_babies_are_born_every_day_in_the_world.

2. J. Vernon McGee, *Thru the Bible with J. Vernon McGee, Vol. 5* (Nashville, Thomas Nelson Publishers, 1983), pg. 1074.

Chapter 39: The First Sixty-Nine Weeks

1. John MacArthur, "Daniel 9 (interpreting Bible prophecy literally)", available both as text and video on YouTube, accessed September 2014, http://www.youtube.come/watch?v=_NkGzWdcgJY&feature=youtube_gdata_player.

Chapter 42: The Abomination of Desolation

1. "2 Maccabees – Catholic Public Domain Version of the Sacred Bible", accessed online at http://www.sacredbible.org/catholic/OT-46_2-Maccabees.htm#5.

Chapter 46: Christ's Victory and Antichrist's Doom

1. John MacArthur, *The MacArthur Study Bible (NKJV)* (Nashville, Word Publishing, 1997), pg. 1250.

Made in the USA
Monee, IL
13 July 2021